CH00952348

RICHARD CROUSE

Raising Hell

KEN RUSSELL AND THE UNMAKING OF
THE DEVILS

ECW PRESS

Copyright © Richard Crouse, 2012

Published by ECW Press
665 Gerrard Street East, Toronto, Ontario, Canada M4M 1Y2
416-694-3348 / info@ecwpress.com

All rights reserved. No part of this publication may be reproduced, stored in a retrieval system, or transmitted in any form by any process — electronic, mechanical, photocopying, recording, or otherwise — without the prior written permission of the copyright owners and ECW Press. The scanning, uploading, and distribution of this book via the Internet or via any other means without the permission of the publisher is illegal and punishable by law. Please purchase only authorized electronic editions, and do not participate in or encourage electronic piracy of copyrighted materials. Your support of the author's rights is appreciated.

Library and Archives Canada Cataloguing in Publication

Crouse, Richard, 1963–
Raising hell : Ken Russell and the unmaking of The Devils / Richard Crouse.

ISBN 978-1-77041-066-4
Also issued as 978-1-77090-280-0 (PDF) and 978-1-77090-281-7 (ePub)

1. Russell, Ken, 1927-2011—Criticism and interpretation.
2. Devils (Motion picture). I. Title.

PN1997.D493C76 2012   791.43'72   C2012-902733-2

Editor for the press: Jennifer Hale
Cover design and illustration: Gary Pullin
Author photo: James Heaslip
Type and production: Rachel Ironstone

The publication of Raising Hell has been generously supported by the Canada Council for the Arts which last year invested $20.1 million in writing and publishing throughout Canada, and by the Ontario Arts Council, an agency of the Government of Ontario. We also acknowledge the financial support of the Government of Canada through the Canada Book Fund for our publishing activities, and the contribution of the Government of Ontario through the Ontario Book Publishing Tax Credit. The marketing of this book was made possible with the support of the Ontario Media Development Corporation.

To Andrea,
my favorite little devil

CONTENTS

Prologue

"GIVE ME MOODY ONE": MY NIGHT WITH KEN RUSSELL

It was the kind of email that sends a chill down your spine. On the day an ad appeared in the newspaper touting my live interview with legendary director Ken Russell at a screening of his cult film *The Devils*, I got a note from Phil Brown, a writer who had just had the "pleasure" of interviewing Russell on the phone. It did not go well. Not well at all. Brown was barely able to coax even "yes" or "no" answers from the cranky eighty-three-year-old.

Here's a taste:

> **Q:** What did you base *The Devils* on and what drew you to the material?
> **Ken Russell:** It was so long ago that I can't remember now.
> **Q:** Do you consider it a horror movie?
> **Ken Russell:** No.

You get the idea. Not promising.

I checked my contract. I'd been hired to interview him for one hour after the movie. Desperation set in. I went online to see if there were any other recent Russell interviews I could read to gauge if he really had nothing to say or was simply having a bad day when he spoke to my colleague.

A quick Google search of the terms "Ken Russell" and "interview" returned some alarming results, several of which referred to the event I was hosting. "Richard Crouse has the unenviable task of interviewing the tight-lipped

Russell," said one search result. Others revealed him to be just as monosyllabic as I feared.

I called the promoter with an idea. Perhaps I should have dinner with Russell before the show to warm him up. Typically I don't like to meet with my interviewees before-hand — I'd rather get them fresh onstage — but in this case it seemed like a good idea. A day or so later I heard back. He'd love to have dinner.

Things were looking up.

The night of the show we met at Southern Accent, just around the corner from the Bloor Cinema in Toronto where the show was being held. I walked past the theater on my way to dinner. There were a few hundred people already waiting outside. A cold sweat enveloped me, even though it was August and sweltering on the street.

At the restaurant we were seated at a large table with the promoter, several members of his entourage, Russell and his wife, Lisi Tribble. I sat next to Russell and introduced myself. He smiled but said nothing. I told him a story about how, as a twelve-year-old child, I snuck out of the house and hitchhiked 200 miles to see *Tommy*, his 1975 rock opera. I told him I was grounded for a year afterward, but it was worth it. He smiled a bit more broadly, but still no sound passed his lips. The waiter came by. Russell's wife ordered him a drink. He smiled.

At least he seemed to be in a good mood.

The waiter came back. More smiles and I thought I detected a nodding of the head but still no words. I was thinking of excusing myself from the table and faking a heart attack to get out of hosting, but I persevered. The silence at the table was deafening so I left early to check out the theater. It was sold out. Even the balcony was jammed. Nine hundred and fifty seats sold to hear my conversation with a mute.

We'd had to move the onstage setup of two chairs and a table to the auditorium floor because Russell wouldn't have been able to make it up the steep stage stairs. Trouble was, we were plunged into darkness down there. Great, I thought, sitting in the dark talking to myself for an hour. This would be the hardest-earned paycheck ever.

My phone rang. Russell was on the way. He moved very slowly, so I was told to chat up the audience before my intro. I told the *Tommy* story. I talk about *The Devils*, how it is one of the most controversial movies ever made and how lucky we were to be seeing it on the big screen. The audience was eating it up. Whooping. Clapping. I still had no idea if Russell was prepared to actually say anything.

I introduced him as he walked down the aisle, supported on one side by his wife, on the other by the promoter who got me into this mess. When the words "Help me welcome Ken Russell" slipped from my mouth, the audience jumped to its feet as though an electric shock was sent through every seat in the place. It was as if I had just said, "Ladies and gentlemen, back from the dead to sing for you tonight, Elvis!"

He nodded his now familiar nod to the audience but said nothing.

I took a deep breath and started with a general question about the film. He answered. Hooray! What he said didn't seem to make much sense, but at least I knew his vocal cords were working. I could work with that.

From there it was as if he fed off the energy of the audience and grew stronger as the night wore on. He was funny, eccentric and slightly cantankerous. Most of all he was long-winded! In short he was just like the movie he was there to speak about — confounding, unexpected and entertaining.

When I asked what made Oliver Reed's performance in *The Devils* so special he said, "It's a rather unique performance insofar as he really pulled out all the stops. I had a special working relationship with him. It was quite simple but very effective. He called me Jesus.

"I directed him in a very simple fashion. He'd say, 'What do you want, Jesus?' and I would say, 'Give me Moody One.' Moody One was one of the simplest instructions that I could give him. Moody Two was a little more important and Moody Three was 'do anything you like.' And that was what we usually did. [Moody Three] could be extremely dangerous. He was a very moody guy and I would often say, 'Careful, boy! There are women and children present.' He would let himself go."

I followed by asking if Reed's unpredictability was what made him a great actor.

"Great actor?" he deadpanned. "I never said he was a great actor. No, he was a terrible actor."

Why did you work with him over and over again?

"'Cause he was cheap. He did the movie thing to perfection and he never let me down, I must say. Once we had worked out Moody One, Moody Two and Moody Three, he was good as gold."

To wrap things up after a wide-ranging discussion about his life and films, someone in the audience asked who the filmmaker he most admired was. Without hesitation he said, "Ken Russell!" Cue the applause.

When it was over, fifty-five minutes later, his assistant hugged me. "He hasn't done an interview like that in years," he said.

✝ ✝ ✝

Writing in *Esquire* Chris Heath said, "It's hard to remember now that there was a time, not just before Netflix but before VHS home video, when most movies were secrets. Movies with special images and weird dissonant ways of looking at the world could usually only be seen with great effort, typically when they came to the one cinema in town that catered to the arty college crowd; even the keenest movie fan might have to wait many years to see every film by a favorite director."

Heath was writing about Werner Herzog, but the words are even truer in regard to Ken Russell. His films, especially *The Devils*, are still hard to find even in the age of On Demand, Netflix and Blu-ray. His work is woefully underrepresented on video store shelves, and unbelievably the full, uncut version of *The Devils* has never been officially released for home consumption. Shoddy bootlegs exist, there's an Asian laser disc and in 2012 a DVD from BFI Video presented the original U.K. X certificate version, but still didn't include the film's controversial moments despite the fact that the fully restored film is reportedly sitting, gathering dust, in a Warner Brothers vault somewhere. Even after four decades the movie is thought to be too controversial for release.

Considering Ken Russell's fame as an auteur at the time of *The Devils* — the *London Observer* listed him as one of England's most influential citizens, ranking him higher than the prime minister, Harold Wilson — it is quite shocking how little was written about the film upon its release or after. Contemporary writers (mostly) wrote it off — stay tuned for some of the most scathing reviews ever — and though interviews appeared in *Time*, *Sight & Sound* and others, surprisingly little ink was spilled on what is, arguably, Russell's greatest film.

Even in his own books — *Directing Film* and *Altered States: The Autobiography* — Russell glosses over the movie, almost as if the pain of documenting its butchering by censors and studios is too much for him to bear.

In conversation that summer evening in 2010, he called it "a great film, and those who haven't seen it are in for a treat." I agree. Murray Melvin, who plays the handsy Father Mignon in the film, was emphatic in May 2011 when he said to me, "Ken physically is not in good health — goodness knows how much longer we'll have him, which will upset us all and it would be wonderful before he goes if those terrible people at Warner's were to release it."

In November 2011, after a release date for a home entertainment version of the film was announced, the *Times* published an article written by Russell, titled "The Return of My Masterpiece," in which he wrote, "I can't help but be thrilled that my film will have its day. We'll turn down the lights, turn on the DVD, my wife will hold my hand and we'll have a blast, waiting for that moment when Reed declaims, 'Satan's boy I could never be!'" Sadly, Russell died of natural causes only five days later, on November 27, 2011, and was denied that moment.

In this book, incorporating new interviews with Russell; editor Michael Bradsell; composer Peter Maxwell Davies; actors Gemma Jones, Judith Paris, Murray Melvin and Dudley Sutton; fans of the film like Guillermo del Toro, Terry Gilliam, Joe Dante, Rod Lurie, Alex Cox, John Landis, William Friedkin, David Cronenberg, Adam Chodzko, Wayne Maginn and Lloyd Kaufman; friends of Russell like Ken Hanke and Leonard Pollack and a host of scholars and experts, like *Rue Morgue*'s Rod Gudiño and *Fangoria*'s Chris Alexander, combined with what little there is out there, I have tried to do justice to the tale of the most controversial movie ever made. Special thanks goes to Andrea Bodnar, Kris Abel, Steve Hayward, Allan Morris Campbell, Seamus O'Regan, the teams from *Canada AM*, *Metro* and NewsTalk 1010 and Jen Hale who helped me form this crazy story into a book and ECW Press for having the courage to release a book about this difficult and challenging movie.

Chapter One

OLIVER REED AND KEN RUSSELL

"Now there's a man well worth going to hell for, aye!" — off-camera voice, *The Devils*

The importance of Ken Russell in Oliver Reed's career was wittily summed up by a gag gift sent by Irish actor Richard Harris to Reed in 1969. The two hell-raising actors carried on a friendly rivalry for years, characterized by outrageous public behavior and personal jabs. Reed had gotten the latest insult in when he joked in the media, "Even though people say Richard Harris and I have been having a great feud, it's not true. After all, how could we be feuding for years? I'd never heard of him until two weeks ago."

In response Harris sent Reed a gift-wrapped pair of Victorian crutches. On one of them the name "Ken Russell" was elaborately inscribed. Attached to the crutch was a note that read, "In my Royal opinion you should not dispense with these, otherwise you will fall flat on your arse." It was a good-natured poke at Reed, whose work and success were so closely associated with the provocative director.

Despite Oliver Reed's family connections — his grandfather Sir Herbert Beerbohm Tree founded the Royal Academy of Dramatic Art — the actor never took formal acting lessons. On the British chat show *Aspel & Company* he explained the nontraditional way he learned his craft:

> I didn't go to acting school. My uncle, who was a director at the time [Sir Carol Reed, the Palme d'Or winner in 1949 for *The Third Man* and the 1968 Academy Award winner for Best Director for *Oliver!*],

said you should go to RADA and you should camp outside directors' lawns in a tent and ask them for a job every time they go to the studio in the morning and that's how you'd get a job. You have to be enthusiastic. But to me, the people who were teaching at RADA were people who can't do it. They might be very good at teaching people to speak English but then I knew how to speak English. My grandfather and my father insisted that we should and I was educated in the south, so I had to work through it in a different way. So pubs and the army were the places where I rubbed shoulders with people I wouldn't normally have rubbed shoulders with and I found them a little bit more interesting than the people I was at school with, so I started to emulate them.

Then along came a new kind of British cinema, a new wave of Angry Young Men who, like Reed, challenged the social status quo. Exemplified by the playwright John Osborne, whose play *Look Back in Anger* was a seminal work of the genre, and actors like Alan Bates, Dirk Bogarde, Tom Courtenay, Albert Finney and Malcolm McDowell, the movement was a slap in the face to the established British art scene. It was kitchen sink drama, showing for the first time the nitty-gritty of everyday British life. It so appealed to Reed that the bullnecked wannabe actor stepped up his training for film work by "getting into fights at pubs." It was this life experience mixed with a natural swagger that defined his early film work.

His first credited film role came in 1960, playing the leader of a gang of violent teddy boys (Brit rockers who dressed in Victorian-style clothes) in the Norman Wisdom comedy *The Bulldog Breed*. (Also appearing is future superstar Michael Caine, who shares a brief scene with Reed in what would be the only time Caine and Reed acted together.) Tough guy bit parts led to larger roles, and in the early '60s Reed glowered through a series of Hammer horror, action and swashbuckling films, which met with varying degrees of success.

In 1960 Reed appeared in roles as diverse as an uncredited tough nightclub bouncer in *The Two Faces of Dr. Jekyll* and a gay ballet dancer in *The League of Gentlemen*. Later that year he was cast as a treacherous thirteenth-century nobleman in the Robin Hood actioner *Sword of Sherwood Forest*. Unfortunately, even though he was featured on the poster in a dramatic pose, his role was altered in post-production. As though he was being punished for being a naughty boy, he is seen but not heard. His voice — complete with a campy French accent — is audible in the trailer but was redubbed by another actor for the theatrical release.

Nonetheless, he considered it an agreeable experience. "It was hide-and-seek with swords," he said, "it was goodies and baddies and damsels in distress and I was Errol Flynn and every other hero I had watched at the cinema."

His first significant role came in 1961. Hammer, the British film studio best known for a twenty-year string of Gothic horror films that spanned the mid-'50s to the '70s, had the rights to remake any of the iconic American monster pictures courtesy of a distribution deal with Universal Pictures. The British company scored big with their version of *The Mummy* and prepped their next reimagining, an adaptation of Guy Endore's novel *The Werewolf of Paris*. Working on a shoestring, they shaped the story to fit Hammer's penny-pinching mold. The story's location was changed from Paris to Spain so the studio could shoot the film back to back on the same sets as the proposed Spanish movie *The Inquisitor*, and an unknown was cast in the lead role.

Chosen from a field of seventeen hopefuls, Reed won the part of Leon in *The Curse of the Werewolf*, a peasant boy whose lycanthropy can only be tamed through love. Reed impressed director Terence Fisher and producer Anthony Hinds with his smoldering intensity and makeup artist Jack Ashton with his face. "[Reed's] powerful bone structure was just right for the appearance and his gifts as an actor were perfect for the part," said Ashton. "In addition, he resembles a wolf anyway when he is very angry."

Reed impresses in one of his best performances for Hammer. His complex take on Leon reveals the character's inner struggle to control his animalistic side while caring for and protecting the people he loves. The tender scenes work, but the performance becomes memorable late in the film when he changes into the beast. The snarling transformation scene is so effective it earned him the nickname "Mr. Scowl."

Despite Reed and the good makeup work, the film fell afoul of censors (scene after scene was excised, reportedly due to the film's lethal mix of horror, sex and even bestiality), critics (one called the movie "a singularly repellant job of slaughter-house horror") and audiences, who stayed away. One unexpected side effect for Hammer was the sudden loss of one of their distribution territories. The Spanish government, so upset by the portrayal of eighteenth-century Spain in the movie, banned all Hammer products for the next fifteen years.

Even though *The Curse of the Werewolf* flopped, Reed's stock rose within Hammer and he was soon working steadily, playing leads in *Paranoiac* and meaty supporting roles in *Pirates of Blood River*, *Captain Clegg* and *The Damned*, opposite Hammer superstars like Christopher Lee and Peter Cushing.

"Everyone told me not to do horror films," he said at the

time, "but all I wanted to do was act." He was honing his craft and picked up pointers from his better-known costars.

"The only reason I started acting in the fashion I do," he told interviewer Michael Parkinson in 1973, "is because I made a film once called *Captain Clegg*. I remember Peter Cushing was in it. [After shooting one day] I was in a car crash. My ex-wife rolled the car over and I squashed [my arm] under a lamppost. I appeared the next day and my arm was actually covered in blood and somebody grabbed me and said, 'Are you all right, Captain Clegg?'

"I said, 'Yes [grabbing his arm and wincing]. I'm all right.' Or something like that, probably over the top because I was hurt.

"Peter Cushing came up to me and said, 'Oliver, remember when you are hurt always go for the understatement. If you're going to say, "Yes, I'm hurt," just say, [face blank, no expression in the voice] "Yes, I'm all right"' — and I've kept that up ever since."

It was the birth of his well-crafted menacing aura — an image supported by his wild off-screen antics and public proclamations like, "My only regret is that I didn't drink every pub dry and sleep with every woman on the planet" — that had him typecast in the role of heavy for most of his professional life.

One director who was able to see past the sneering exterior was Ken Russell, a photographer who, like his contemporary Stanley Kubrick, turned to filmmaking. His specialty was genre-busting arts biographies for the BBC.

Ken Russell's first taste of show business came in front of a ballet barre, not behind a camera.

After winning a scholarship to London's International

Ballet School — "[I] was always spraining ankles because I started [dancing] too late, started at twenty-one when most people are finishing" — and after a production of *Annie Get Your Gun*, he left dance behind when his troupe went bankrupt. He was twenty-seven years old and at loose ends, dreaming of a career in film but "it was a closed shop when I was trying. I wrote to all the studios and I got the feeling [that] unless you knew someone who was a cameraman or a clapperboy, why should they give you a job? It's not like today when you can just press a red button and prove to someone you've either got it or you haven't. It was too expensive."

Instead he took up photography, and while he rarely ever made more than five quid a picture, he freelanced, married one of his models and worked steadily. He rarely did studio work: "They only wanted straight fashion against a white backdrop which didn't interest me and I wasn't terribly good at it. I wasn't very good at talking to the fashion models. I didn't have the gift of the gab." Instead he roamed the streets of post–World War II London snapping street people in real, and later in unreal, situations.

He found beauty among the rubble, photographing teddy girls and local people going about their business (one photo of two men on bicycles was later captioned "The answer to the Suez fuel crisis"), but soon his avant-garde tendencies got the best of him. He found himself staging a wedding with street kids on Portobello Road ("Ask your mum for some funny old clothes she don't want," he told them. "Let's imagine we're all grown up and you two are going to get married") and outfitting models in skirts made of lampshades.

"In a way I was making still films," he said, "I suppose, of images."

Even though his strange brand of art photography

was catching on, he remained more interested in the moving image. "Don't forget I saw more films than anyone in England, maybe in the world, by the time I was twenty-one. I was beaten when I went to Pangbourne Nautical College. I used to break bounds to go and see Dorothy Lamour in Reading and I was caught and beaten for it and it was well worth it."

His obsession with movies manifested itself in the form of short amateur films. *Amelia and the Angel*, the story of a young girl who wanders the streets of London searching to replace the damaged costume angel wings she is supposed to wear in her school nativity play, is the best known. Starring the nine-year-old daughter of the Uruguayan ambassador to London — who only agreed to appear in the film after Russell promised her a high-speed tour of the city — the film shows many of Russell's future themes in embryonic form: sin, redemption and Catholicism. It won several awards and spelled the end of Russell's photography career when BBC producer Huw Wheldon saw the film and, impressed, offered Russell his first professional filmmaking job.

"Once I got into films I never thought, 'I wonder what happened to the negatives,'" he said of his days as a photographer. "I just lost total interest."

For the next eleven years — 1959 to 1970 — he made arts documentaries for the BBC series *Monitor* (where he replaced John *Midnight Cowboy* Schlesinger as resident director) and *Omnibus*. Of *Monitor*, Russell said, "Every other Sunday evening at 9:30 the TV screen glowed a little brighter."

Not surprisingly Russell soon earned a reputation as an iconoclast, changing the way the BBC presented documentaries. Among his innovations were longer running times (his doc on composer Edward Elgar was the longest film the BBC had shown on a musician to date), the inclusion of reenactments and the use of actors to portray historical figures at different ages (think Cate Blanchett, Heath Ledger and Richard Gere all playing various incarnations of Bob Dylan in *I'm Not There*) instead of photograph stills and documentary footage. "I think the films finally cleared the air of all the dreary, reverential, schoolmasterly treatments that the word documentary implied," said Russell.

Perhaps his most controversial BBC film was *Dance of the Seven Veils*, which portrayed Richard Strauss as a Nazi. The film so enraged the Strauss family that they withdrew music rights, effectively banishing the film to the delete bin of history. It was the first time the director had faced crippling censorship, but would not be the last.

Inside the mother corp, he quickly gained a reputation as a difficult director. "I had heard that Ken was a rather shy, incommunicative man who was also a bit of a back-seat driver," recalled Michael Bradsell, who edited a trio of highly acclaimed BBC docs with Russell. After breaking the director "of his rather suspicious habits," Bradsell went on to edit eight of Russell's features, including *The Devils*.

Russell remained steadily working at the BBC, only occasionally stepping away to make a feature like *French Dressing*, a 1963 comedy loosely based on Roger Vadim's *And God Created Woman*. It was on a BBC project in 1965 that he first encountered the actor who would become his most frequent on-screen collaborator.

Russell had planned on filming his take on the story of French composer Claude Debussy for the big screen, but the financial failure of *French Dressing* made raising the necessary funds impossible so he retreated into the open arms of the BBC with the project. Co-written with Melvyn Bragg, the script owes a nod to Fellini and his classic *8½* in its surreal approach to biography.

The pair created an ingenious nonlinear scenario layering in three tiers of storytelling. Merging fiction and reality, they included a dramatized retelling of the composer's fiery life and relationships, visualizations of his music (including the disquieting image of Saint Sebastian pierced point blank with arrows) and finally a film-within-a-film about a director making a movie about Debussy's life to create a documentary unlike anything before seen on the BBC.

"Debussy was an ambiguous character and I always let the character of the person or his work dictate the way the film goes," Russell said. "Also, one was a bit critical of artists like Debussy and I thought the time had come to ask questions, and the natural way for me to ask questions was to have a film director talking to an actor, because an actor always asks questions about the character he's playing and the director usually had to answer them, or try to, often just to keep him happy. And when I found that Debussy was friendly with an intellectual named Pierre Louÿs from whom he derived a lot, it seemed an analogous relationship to that of a film director and an actor."

Now to find a leading man.

At this point in his career the twenty-seven-year-old Oliver Reed was fighting against the typecasting that kept him firmly entrenched in bad-guy roles. "I had the misfortune to look like a prizefighter and speak like a public school boy," he said. "When I started, the only jobs I got were as teddy boys in leather jackets who whipped old ladies around the head with a bicycle chain and stole their handbags."

Wanting to branch out, he figured he needed one role that could prove he was capable of more than glowering on command. Enter Ken Russell, who arranged an audition with Reed in the BBC office Russell shared with three other directors. According to Cliff Goodwin's book *Evil Spirits*, the meeting went something like this:

"I hear you're considering me for Debussy," said Reed when the men met face to face.

"Do you know anything about Debussy?" replied Russell, sizing up the actor.

"Not a thing."

As Russell gave Reed a *Reader's Digest* version of the composer's life a bored look formed on the actor's face. Russell then abruptly wrapped the meeting with a curt "Well, thanks for coming in."

"So I won't be playing the part, then?" Reed asked.

"What do you mean?" Russell asked, confused.

"Is it this?" Reed asked, jutting out his chin to emphasize the facial scars he had earned in a bar fight the year before.

"I didn't see anything," said Russell, who had been immediately struck by Reed's broodiness and his physical resemblance to Debussy. "So do you want to do the film?"

"Yeah, sure," said Reed.

He hemmed and hawed before signing on officially, concerned that the BBC paycheck didn't match the money he had been earning in feature films. For advice he contacted Michael Winner, a filmmaker and friend. "I told him to go for it," Winner told Goodwin years later. "Ken Russell was a director he should get close to."

As for Russell, no convincing was necessary. "When I first saw him he looked terrific," he said. "He struck me as vivacious, cheeky and not run-of-the-mill. I remember him being very moody and glowering. I liked his spirit. Everyone else I auditioned seemed to fade into insignificance."

Part of the film was shot in Chalon-sur-Saône, a small French commune best known as the birthplace of photography. The shoot, however, was almost scuttled when French customs confiscated the production's costumes and makeup.

Rather than turn tail, however, Russell pressed on, adapting the cast and crew's personal wardrobes and buying makeup in local pharmacies.

The French shoot, despite a rocky start, was a success but even the wrap party was subject to the Beeb's tight purse strings. Russell booked a table for a nine-person crew lunch only to discover that the wine, at nine pounds, was out of his expense account's price range. Rather than leave, Russell and Reed went down the street, bought a dozen bottles of cheaper wine and smuggled them into the restaurant. When the one official bottle of house hooch emptied they simply refilled it under the table with their BBC-approved wine. It was the first of much flamboyant tomfoolery the pair indulged in and bonded over.

The role — in which Reed played the dual parts of Debussy and the actor who plays him in the film-within-the-film — wasn't that much of a stretch for the actor, who once again relied on his natural swagger to tell the tale, but it had more cachet than a Hammer horror film, was more ambitious in scope than the movies he had been making and exposed him to a wider audience. "[*The Debussy Film*] was the point at which I began to shoot upwards," Reed said of the career boost the film gave him.

It also began the most fruitful artistic collaboration of Reed's career. Although with director Michael Winner he had made six films over twenty-five years and enjoyed considerable commercial success, it was his work with Russell that defined Reed's career and, for the most part, represented professional highs. "Winner gave me my bread and Russell gave me my art," Reed said.

The two men meshed on-screen and off, blazing a trail that pushed personal excess and cinematic experimentation to the fore. The off-screen shenanigans of the two men could fill a book, but the extreme nature of their relationship is detailed in this quotation from a 2007 column Russell wrote for the *Sunday Times* about filming a medieval duel between him and his lead actor:

> This came about when we were rehearsing a scene for a film about Thomas à Becket he wished me to direct [the unproduced *The King's Man*]. I was standing in for the Archbishop of Canterbury, on top of a wooden chest doubling up for the cathedral altar. I was armed with a trusty, rusty broadsword almost as tall as I was. Playing a renegade knight, Oliver prepared to let fly at me with a dagger, murder in his eyes. I knew I had to stop him or die. It wasn't a joke. With Oliver, you didn't joke. Sweating, I raised my heavy broadsword as Oliver launched himself at me. I waited and waited, then brought down the sword at the last possible moment. There was a ripping of material. Oliver's shirt started to turn crimson. The blade had delicately bisected the shirtfront.
>
> Oliver tore the shirt apart, strode to the mantelpiece, lifted the glass dome from a pair of stuffed pheasants, tossed the birds on the fire, then, wiping his bloody chest with the stained shirt, placed the remnants under the glass dome and turned to face me. "It'll stay there till my dying day," he said, smiling proudly.

Writing in his autobiography *A British Picture*, Russell brings the fight into sharp focus: "Everything was a game to Oliver and must be played by two simple rules. The game must be played in deadly earnest and it must be played to the end, whatever the outcome. Any infringement of the rules incurs not only Oliver's displeasure but, what is worse, his contempt."

In total Reed and Russell worked together nine times

(including fleeting and well-disguised cameo appearances in *Mahler* and *Lisztomania*, although one that got away was *A Clockwork Orange*, which Russell was thinking of making with Reed). On the heels of *The Debussy Film* Reed narrated *Always on Sunday*, a bio-pic on the French painter Henri Rousseau, and starred as nineteenth-century artist and poet Dante Gabriel Rossetti in *Dante's Inferno: The Private Life of Dante Gabriel Rossetti, Poet and Painter* (another BBC film, described as containing moments of "inspired lunacy"). It was during the making of the latter that the pair developed their unique system of shorthand communication of "Moody One" and "Moody Two."

Cast member Judith Paris remembered that the two men shared more than just a spiritual connection. "[Ken] and Oliver were like twins," she said. "There was a moment I remember when we were doing Rossetti [*Dante's Inferno*] where Oliver and he walked off to discuss a shot and you couldn't tell the two of them apart in the distance. They both had long legs and short bodies and a mass of dark, curly hair and round faces. They looked like twin brothers talking to each other. It was quite extraordinary."

It wasn't until 1969's *Women in Love*, however, that their collaboration caused controversy and critical raves in equal measure. Reed had starred in the first film to include the word "fuck" (*I'll Never Forget What's'isname*), as well as the first British film to be rated X due to its violent content (*Sitting Target*), but it was the famous nude wrestling scene between Reed and co-star Alan Bates — another cinematic first — that catapulted *Women in Love*, Russell and Reed to the front page.

"You know *Women in Love* couldn't have been financed without my name," said Reed. "I had acted in the television programs of Debussy and Rossetti for Russell. *Women in Love* was a sort of thank-you film."

The film is an adaptation of D.H. Lawrence's racy 1920 novel of sexual torment. Now cited as one of the 100 best English-language novels of the twentieth century by the Modern Library, the book was labeled filth upon release. "Dirt in heaps," said one critic, "festering, putrid heaps which smell to high Heaven."

Depicting the relationships between the elite of Britain's industrial Midlands — played by Alan Bates, Reed (in the role Michael Caine turned down), Glenda Jackson and Jennie Linden — during the early part of the twentieth century, the film was bound to be controversial as well but Reed's insistence on staying faithful to the book pushed the movie into the realm of the truly contentious.

In a 2007 column on adaptations for the *Sunday Times* Russell described how the star persuaded him to film the scene as it appeared in the book, censors be damned.

> In *Women in Love* we decided that, discretion being the better part of valor, perhaps we should relocate the nude wrestling scene from a cozy interior in a stately home to a moonlit meadow at night and close to a stream (into which our naked men could tumble, thus hiding a multitude of censorable sins).
>
> But we reckoned without the opinion of one of the male leads — Oliver Reed, who hammered on my front door one night as I was sitting down to dine. "She says it's not like that in the book," he said, bursting into the room and nodding to a shadowy female figure behind him. "She says they wrestle in the dining room, not some tacky field in the moonlight."
>
> "It would never pass the censor. Anyway, it's implausible," I said, as he moved toward me . . .

"You'll live to thank me for this, Jesus," Reed crowed after literally beating the reticent director over the head to shoot the scene his way. Russell later referred to the violent incident as a "script conference."

The resulting balls-to-the-wall nude wrestling match between two men — which took three days and many bottles of vodka to shoot in a purportedly haunted house called Elvaston Castle in Derbyshire — was unlike any fight scene on film to date. It sent shock waves through audiences who had never before seen male frontal nudity at their local Bijou. "Yes, I suppose it was the first time you actually got to see the actual star's actual organs," said star Alan Bates.

In fact, the scene as originally shot was even more revealing, but at the request of U.K. censor John Trevelyan — who called the nude wrestling scene "remarkably brilliant" — Russell altered the rough edit, excising some full-length shots of the nude men standing motionless before the fight begins and darkening the intensity of the sunlight streaming into the room. Other than that, the scene played as shot, earning it an uncut X certificate. From 1951 to 1970 the X certificate was applied to films deemed suitable for audiences sixteen years and older by the British Board of Film Censors. It replaced the H certificate, which had primarily been assigned to horror films between the years 1932 and 1951. In 1970 the age limit was bumped up to 18, where it remains, although since 1982 the rating has been known as Restricted 18. (Decades later another film, with a similar nude wrestling scene, *Borat: Cultural Learnings of America for Make Benefit Glorious Nation of Kazakhstan*, would earn an R rating for pervasive, strong, crude and sexual content including graphic nudity and language, even though they blocked out the genitalia with large black bars.)

"We had little criticism," wrote Trevelyan in his book

What the Censor Saw, "possibly because of the film's undoubted brilliance."

"I've always been a great reader of Lawrence," said Bates, "and the wrestling [was] really what Lawrence was all about. Physical contact. Contact with the earth, contact with the ground, contact with each other — expressed physically, not only sexually. The point of discussion about that fight is — yes, it's got sexual undertones, but it's first and foremost a physical contact, as an expression of need or of friendship. A need to expand yourself. The reason they fight is because each of them is in a particular extreme state in his life. They both lived in a very constricted society. And to me that kind of explosion, although it's got an intellectual side to it too, is a natural thing. It's extreme, but it's not unnatural."

The buff and tumble scene was scissored almost entirely in South America, cutting after Gerald (Reed) locked the door and picking up with the two men lying on the floor panting, leaving what happened in between to the viewers' imaginations. "It became known as the Great Buggering Scene and filled the cinemas for months," said Russell. "So much for the subtleties of censorship."

Interestingly, years later Russell described how an audience of pensioners in the early 2000s were unaffected by the nudity. When Bates and Reed's famous scene came on the screen one of the old folks turned to the other and said, "Nice carpet," noting the décor rather than the ding-dongs.

Audiences appreciated the film, even if the British critics didn't. "They should take all the pretentious dialogue out of the soundtrack," wrote one critic, "and call it *Women in Heat*." Reed was unfazed by the bad hometown reviews and so were audiences, who flocked to the film, breaking box office records.

Stateside reviews were glowing — "a visual stunner and very likely the most sensuous film ever made," wrote the *New*

York Daily News — and the following year Glenda Jackson won a Best Actress Academy Award for her work as Gudrun Brangwen, becoming the first to win the award for a role that had a nude scene, a role she later revisited when she made 1989's *The Rainbow* and played the mother of the character she had played twenty years earlier in *Women in Love*.

Jackson, a RADA–trained actress, didn't tell Russell she was pregnant until well into shooting for fear she would be fired. She must have been surprised when the director reacted favorably to the news. Pleased with her performance, he suggested they postpone her nude scenes until later in the production schedule so her breasts would be larger. "I was five months pregnant when I made that nude scene in *Women in Love*," she said. "I'd never had such a marvelous bosom."

For Reed, the film cemented his reputation as not only a serious actor, but as a box office draw. So much so that he was seriously considered as Sean Connery's replacement in the James Bond franchise, but was ruled out by producer Albert R. "Cubby" Broccoli because of his boozy reputation. Broccoli wrote in a letter, "With Reed we would have had a far greater problem to destroy his image and remold him as James Bond. We just didn't have the time or money to do that."

For Russell, the movie placed him on the very short list of international directors with box office pull.

After completing *Women in Love*, Reed and Russell went their separate ways — temporarily. Russell worked on *The Lonely Heart* (later renamed *The Music Lovers*), a baroque bio of nineteenth-century Russian composer Pyotr Ilyich Tchaikovsky, which he described as "the story of the marriage between a homosexual and a nymphomaniac." Based on *Beloved Friend*, a collection of personal correspondence edited by Catherine Drinker Bowen and Barbara von Meck, the idiosyncratic script was penned by frequent Russell collaborator Melvyn Bragg. The movie reunited Russell with Glenda Jackson, but his leading man this time out was Richard Chamberlain, who for four years was network TV's leading hunk as Dr. James Kildare on the eponymous series.

"Well, I'd just completed *Julius Caesar* at Elstree Studios with Charlton Heston and Robert Vaughn," said Chamberlain. "In actual fact, I was all set to catch a jet back home when Ken Russell called me. I thought the idea behind the film so different that I just had to say yes!"

Like several of Russell's other music bios, *The Music Lovers* (1970) is presented mostly without dialogue; instead it's a fever dream, using flashbacks, nightmares and fantasy sequences set to Tchaikovsky's music. "It tells the story of one of the incidents in Tchaikovsky's life that he might have liked to forget," said Russell, "but, you know, that was part of his story, and so I followed his ups and downs throughout his career."

Russell weaves a wild, "maximalist" portrait of the musician, illustrating the scars left behind by his mother's horrible death — she was drowned in scalding water in a cholera cure gone wrong — and how his marriage was torn apart by the composer's torment over his homosexual urges toward Count Anton Chiluvsky (Christopher Gable).

"It's an intimate version, dealing with the man as much as with his music," said Chamberlain before shooting commenced, "and he will be seen as a homosexual. It deals with his marriage and his relationship with Madame Von Meck and his close male friend, to be played by Christopher Gable — he was a lead dancer with the Royal Ballet before he became an actor. The homosexuality is not dwelt on, but, you know."

Eventually Tchaikovsky's mental health deteriorates and when he loses von Meck's patronage, he dies of cholera. "It's a horrible death and you will see it," said Chamberlain. "He died ten days after conducting the *Pathétique* symphony for the first time. Recently, in Russia, they discovered that he deliberately drank some unboiled water and this caused his death."

Where other movie bios of classical composers, like the majestic *Amadeus* or the slick *Immortal Beloved*, are buffed and polished entertainments, *The Music Lovers* is raw, surrealistic, filled with anxiety and indulgence. It peels back the layers of history to reveal the person, and the quirks of his creative genius.

The cherry on top, of course, is Russell's wild Grand Guignol style. As the characters become more extreme so does the look of the film, as if the audacious director is trying to out-Fellini Fellini. Most notorious is the expressionist sequence set to Tchaikovsky's most well-known work, *1812 Overture*, described by one writer as a "visualization of madness." It is certainly the product of a director working near the top of his form.

The movie was hailed and reviled in equal measure. In *Life* Richard Schickel praised the film, writing that Russell is "a man drunk on the power of film, on his own masterful and manic command of the medium." Others went on the attack. *New York Times* writer Vincent Canby said, "Mr. Russell has told us a lot less about Tchaikovsky and his music than he has about himself as a filmmaker." Dave Kehr of the *Chicago Reader* gave the movie a backhanded compliment, noting Glenda Jackson's performance while suggesting she is the only "actress who can hold her own against Russell's excess."

"Of course [the picture] was excessive, crude, flamboyant," answered Russell. "That was what fascinated me about the subject, the excessive romanticism. There seems to be a general distrust of freely expressed emotion these days — a feeling that there's a virtue in understatement; I don't believe that."

Russell essayist Thomas R. Atkins gets the final word. In the Monarch Film Studies book devoted to Ken Russell he wrote, "If one can forget categories like 'musical biography' or even 'biography' and look at the film for what it seems to be — a serious study of sexuality, with Tchaikovsky used as the focus of the study — the effect of the totality is quite different from what the critics suggest."

Meanwhile Oliver Reed was busy forging his reputation as Mr. England. Despite offers to leave the U.K. and set up shop in Los Angeles, Reed stayed put. "I'm not going," he said. "I'm a Brit and I'm staying here." Few of the European films he made during this period — like the drama *The Lady in the Car with Glasses and a Gun* and the romantic comedy *Take a Girl Like You* — made much of an impact outside the U.K. Certainly not as much as the American films he was being offered and rejecting at the same time.

Richard Zanuck, producer and son of one of the architects of the Hollywood studio system Darryl F. Zanuck, was keen to work with the British superstar and offered him plum roles in two movies that became classics — *The Sting* and *Jaws*.

Both offers met with a resounding no and both roles went to another Brit, Robert Shaw. Reed's brother (and sometimes press agent) surmised that his brother would have felt as though he was "tarting himself around" by going to Hollywood: "It may not have had a lot of logic for most people, but it had a raw logic for him."

Decades later Reed rued the decision. "Ultimately I ended up making obscure European films that paid well," he said, "but did nothing to further my reputation."

Around this time, in 1969, Ken Russell submitted a script to censor John Trevelyan for perusal. He wanted to know if the draft contained censorable scenes or themes. Trevelyan's brow must have furrowed as he wrote a letter to Russell detailing the "numerous items I felt would almost certainly need to be censored."

"There is no way [Sister Jeanne] can say 'cunt.'"

Russell, who based his script on the Aldous Huxley book *The Devils of Loudun* and the 1960 play *The Devils* by John Whiting, had no idea he was prepping a film that would become one of the most controversial movies ever made. And he clearly didn't know how prophetic he was being when he said, "I want to upset people, to make them react to what they see."

Chapter Two

INSPIRATION AND THE WRITING

"I also have a maxim, Father: give me three lines of a man's handwriting and I will hang him." — Baron de Laubardemont, *The Devils*

Located about twenty miles south of the town of Chinon and fifteen miles east of the town of Thouars, Loudun is a commune in the Vienne department in the Poitou-Charentes region in western France. The town was known as the home of the great grammarian Scévole de Sainte-Marthe (whose fame enticed Charles I of England to visit) and for a devastating outbreak of the plague in the summer of 1632, which claimed 3,700 of the town's population of 14,000. More recently it has been known as the hometown of Nicolas Ghesquière, creative director of the French fashion house Balenciaga. But Loudun will always be most famous for a series of possessions that happened in 1634.

The alleged demonic possession of the Ursuline nuns in seventeenth-century Loudun is probably the most notorious case of mass possession in history. Twenty-seven nuns claimed to be possessed, obsessed or bewitched by Father Urbain Grandier, the walled city's priest in the church of Sainte-Croix. In actuality the case of demonic possession was a politically motivated ruse to remove Grandier from his post. The "bewitched" nuns were more likely possessed by mass hysteria and fear of the witch hunters and exorcists who showed up to investigate than by any supernatural force, but nonetheless, they put on quite a show. Aldous Huxley wrote in *The Devils of Loudun* (1952), "At first the nuns observed the most perfect decorum; but at the moment of communion, the Prioress, Soeur Claire and Soeur Agnès went into convulsions and rolled on the floor, howling obscenities and blasphemies. The rest of the community followed suit and for an hour or two the church looked like a mixture between a bear-garden and a brothel."

During the exorcisms, Sister Jeanne claimed that she and the other nuns were possessed by the demons Asmodeus and Zabulon. The demons, she said, were sent to the nuns when Father Grandier tossed a bouquet of roses over the convent walls.

According to the *Encyclopedia of Demons and Demonology* by Rosemary Ellen Guiley, "The torments of Mother Superior Jeanne des Anges (Joan of the Angels) and the sisters by the handsome Grandier resulted in not only the priest's fiery death [he was burned at the stake] but great debate on the veracity of the nuns' sufferings, the theological probability of witchcraft and the possibility that Grandier had been sacrificed for his political missteps."

Grandier's death did not bring an end to the possessions in Loudun. The commune became a tourist attraction, and the nuns' wild gyrations were put on display twice a day, except on Sunday. The poor possessed nuns would bend over backward, walk on their hands and be pseudo-exorcised by Father Mignon and others.

The shows continued until 1637 when Cardinal Richelieu's niece reported the goings-on to her uncle. He cut off the performers' salaries and shut down the scam. Historians argue over the cause of the mass possession. It's theorized that the entire affair was a hoax orchestrated by Richelieu to unseat Grandier and convert the town's Protestant population to Catholicism.

In 1866 the founder of modern neurology Jean-Martin Charcot suggested that the nuns' behavior was due to hystero-demonopathy. The French neurologist theorized that they were sexually frustrated and had turned their erotic desires into dreams of demonic possession by the handsome Grandier.

Ten years after Grandier was burned at the stake, Sister Jeanne wrote about the experience of being possessed.

> In most cases I saw quite clearly that I was the prime cause of my turmoil and that the demon only acted according to the openings I gave him.
>
> When I spoke of that to my exorcists, they told me it was the demon who gave me those feelings in order to hide within me, or to cast me into a little despair at seeing myself in so much malignancy. I was not the more satisfied for that, for although I submitted to believing what they were telling me at the time, nevertheless my conscience, which was my judge, gave me no peace. Thus all their assurances blinded me. I think the fact is that it was difficult for them to believe that I was so wicked, and that they believed the devils were giving me these scruples . . .
>
> To make myself better understood, I must give a few examples, both in important things and light matters, so that those who may read this will know how necessary it is that souls beleaguered by demons should hold firmly to God and greatly beware of themselves.
>
> It so happened, to my great embarrassment, that during the first days when Father Lactance was given to me to be my director and exorcist, I disapproved of his way of conducting many small matters, although it was a very good way; but it was because I was wicked.
>
> One day he undertook to have us all take communion at our grille.

At that time, since we were for the most part sorely afflicted with the inner turmoil and great convulsions, for the reception of the Eucharist the priest would either come into our chancel or have us go out to take communion in the church. I was angry that he wanted to introduce a different practice. I began to murmur about in my heart, and thought within myself that he would do better to follow the way of the other priests.

As I dwelled negligently on that thought, it entered my mind that, to humiliate that father, the demon would have committed some irreverence toward the Very Holy Sacrament. I was so miserable that I did not resist that thought strongly enough. When I went to take communion, the devil seized my head, and after I had received the holy host and had half moistened it, the devil threw it into the priest's face. I know perfectly well that I did not perform that act freely, but I am very sure, to my great embarrassment, that I gave the devil occasion to do it, and that he would not have had this power had I not allied myself with him.

Over 300 years later, British author Aldous Huxley first heard about the possessions at Loudun. Best known for his futuristic novel *Brave New World* and for giving Jim Morrison the inspiration for his band's name through his novel *The Doors of Perception*, Huxley discussed how he became aware of the strange goings-on at Loudun in a 1961 interview with John Chandos.

Years and years ago I read the account in [Jules] Michelet's book *La Sorcière* of the Loudun case, and was interested — and incidentally found, when I came to look into the documents, that it was extraordinarily inaccurate; this great historian was very slapdash — and then I thought no more about it for many years. Then quite by chance I picked up in a second-hand bookshop the . . . reprint . . . of the autobiography of the prioress and one of [Father] Surin's autobiographical things, and the late seventeenth-century book by [Pastor] Aubin, which is an account of the whole episode. And reading those I was so fascinated — there was such extraordinary material there that I began collecting it, and found in fact that no historical episode yet has had so much documentation. There are autobiographical statements by the prioress, by Surin; a great many letters; all the exorcisms were taken down in shorthand, and a great many of them were printed.

Then there were a great many accounts by outsiders who came to look at the possessions — Loudun became one of the most popular tourist resorts of the seventeenth century. People went from all over the continent to see these nuns rolling on the floor and screaming obscenities — it was the greatest fun.

The historical accounts were one thing, but the thing that makes Huxley's book so valuable and so entertaining is the way he contextualizes the story.

"Here is a story which is strictly historical," said Huxley, "and I really never departed from the historical documents — which is at the same time a parable. And this is what I'm looking for: a historical or biographical medium in terms of which I can think about all sorts of general subjects. I do strongly feel that philosophical and religious ideas are better expressed not in abstract terms but in terms of concrete case histories . . . if you can find the right kind of case history."

The resulting social-psychological interpretation of the true tale is more than just a history book. While the facts of the case are laid end to end in an interesting way, Huxley expands on the themes of the story, contrasting historical views of the leading philosophies of the day to the concerns of his day; the witch-trial mentality becomes a critique of the McCarthy hearings.

In his book *Directing Film*, Russell wrote, "As you may remember if you ever read *Doors of Perception*, Huxley was no stranger to the drug experience himself, and his documentary novel *The Devils of Loudun* is just about the trippiest version of a historical event it has ever been my good fortune to happen upon."

The book, though not well known among Huxley's work, demonstrates the scope of his talents as historian, storyteller, philosopher, social critic and researcher. Called the "peak achievement of Huxley's career" by the *New York Times*, this study of sexual hysteria was labeled "brilliant" by the *Los Angeles Times*: "Huxley's genius at its best: it's his scientific, almost forensic and detailed approach that makes us feel the truth and horror of what happened long ago in France." Reviews notwithstanding, the book did not fly off the shelves. But despite apathy from readers, dramatists recognized the core of a great, theatrical story.

At the center of the book is Urbain Grandier, who served as a Catholic priest in the church of Sainte-Croix in Loudun in the Diocese of Poitiers. He was a complicated man. In *Historic Ghosts and Ghost Hunters*, H. Addington Bruce describes him as "frank and ardent and generous, and . . . idolized by the people of Loudun. But he had serious failings." A contemporary writer, Ismael Boulliau, said, "He had great virtues, but accompanied by great vices, human vices nevertheless, and natural to man." In other words, he was a horndog.

In the Urbain Grandier volume of the *Celebrated Crimes* series, the *Count of Monte Cristo* author Alexandre Dumas describes him thus: "Urbain, who in his intercourse with his friends was cordial and agreeable, was sarcastic, cold and haughty to his enemies. When he had once resolved on a course, he pursued it unflinchingly; he jealously exacted all the honour due to the rank at which he had arrived, defending it as though it were a conquest; he also insisted on enforcing all his legal rights, and he resented the opposition and angry words of casual opponents with a harshness which made them his lifelong enemies."

One high-level enemy was the powerful Cardinal Richelieu. Grandier had both published and publicly spoken scathing criticisms against the chief minister of France. The result was a politically motivated witch hunt (literally) against Grandier led by Richelieu and his allies, who used the priest's philandering lifestyle and bold affairs with women to impeach him. The strongest evidence came from the mother superior of the Ursuline nuns, Sister Jeanne of the Angels. Sister Jeanne, who was sexually obsessed with the priest and felt jilted when he refused to become the spiritual director of the convent, accused him of using black magic to send the demon Asmodeus, among others, to seduce her and twenty-seven other nuns. That the nuns were cloistered and had never met the priest was incidental to the case. Despite a paucity of hard evidence, and the fact that he never confessed to witchcraft despite suffering some of the worst tortures imaginable, Grandier was found guilty and burned at the stake in the town square.

Aside from this protagonist, the story of Loudun had villains, violence, sex, torture and a bunch of crazy nuns. It was perfect fodder for stage and screen at a time when both theater and film were pushing the envelope. Huxley, however, felt the material might be too "powerful" with visuals added to his words. It may have been residue of the sting from the contemporary reviews the book received — in assessments that predicted the write-ups Ken Russell would receive, many critics condemned Huxley's book as offensive. Perhaps it was his disillusionment with Hollywood that led him to spurn offers to adapt it for the screen, or maybe he truly felt it was unfilmable. The author had a deep understanding of the story as well as the mechanics of screenwriting, having penned four produced screenplays (among his films was an adaptation of Jane Austen's *Pride and Prejudice*, which starred young Laurence Olivier), but when Huxley wrote his son, Matthew, about a proposed film version (which predated Russell's version), he had some qualms.

"[T]here is to be a film of *The Devils of Loudun*," he wrote. "What on earth will they make of it? I feel a great deal of curiosity — and some apprehension."

Even when Sir Peter Hall of the Royal Shakespeare Company commissioned British dramatist John Whiting to adapt the book for the stage, Huxley remained conflicted. After reading a rough draft of the play in 1960, he wrote of his concerns to Whiting: "I have just finished your script of *The Devils*, and I find most of it poetical and powerfully dramatic. Indeed, I wonder if some of the scenes in the last two acts may not prove almost too powerful. The possession, exorcism and torture episodes were hair-raising enough in the narrative (incidentally, I exaggerated nothing; everything in the book is drawn from original sources). Dramatized and well directed and acted, they may be almost more than many people can take. In any case, it will be very interesting to see how an audience reacts to the horror and strangeness of the story."

Later in the same letter he says that the main hurdle of the adaptation was finding a way to "prevent the piece from becoming too frightful or too extravagantly indecent and blasphemous."

Whiting was an unusual choice to adapt Huxley's book. A playwright and critic, he was a minor figure and the whipping boy of Britain's new drama wave. His show *Saint's Day* was reviewed by *The Times* as a play "of a badness that must be called indescribable," and he had virtually retired from the stage after the critical drubbing and flop of his 1956 work *The Gates of Summer*. For the last three years of his life, he, ironically, was the theater critic of the *London Magazine*.

By the time Whiting's play, by this time called simply *The Devils*, opened at the Aldwych Theatre in London on February 20, 1961, several liberties had been taken with Huxley's text, in both tone and substance. To smooth out the narrative for the stage, the playwright squeezed the story, shortening the time span between Father Urbain Grandier's arrival in Loudun and his eventual burning at the stake; mixed and matched scenes — juxtaposing, for example, Grandier's torture scene with Prioress Jeanne's confession monologue — and added a one-man Greek chorus — a sewer worker (strange, because no drains existed in 1634 Loudun). He also removed characters and used character composites of historical figures.

Also different from Huxley is the subtext. The basic facts are the same, but Whiting excised allusions to the modern day to focus on Grandier's fixation on self-destruction. Whiting explained:

> The story is essentially simple. A rakish and libertine priest of great charm, high intelligence — well, he wasn't but I made him so — has his women, his power. He is handsome, reasonably rich, and up at the convent there is this lunatic, this crazy mother, who

suddenly begins to have terrible ideas that Beelzebub is lodged in her stomach, or in her lower bowel, or something like that, and is speaking with the voice of the priest. The situation is simply that local superstition — politics, fear, revenge — all subscribe to the fact that people come to believe it, and he is arrested, tried and burned. Now, that's all it is. Well, I mean this could all be out, down, on half a page.

But the thing is a play, somebody's got to say something and therefore one has got to find the significant points in it and a shape. Where do you start? Well, I have started in the gutter, literally in the gutter, and the play gets up out of it. That's the overall shape but how do you do it? You have to have a series of steps. Now these steps again are not important, except to the very few people who will want to know how these things are written. The public is not concerned with the finesse of making a play or a chair or anything else. It merely wants a serviceable article which will do a certain thing — and that can be anything, it can frighten them or stimulate them or work them into a frenzy of rage: all these things are perfectly acceptable.

Reviews were kind, although critics were hardly worked into any kind of frenzy. After a quick rewrite shortly before Whiting died of cancer in 1963, the play ran on Broadway (starring Anne Bancroft and Jason Robards) for thirty-one performances — critic Daniel J. Singal called it "too intellectual for Broadway and too epic for anywhere else" — and again at the Mark Taper Forum in Los Angeles, with Frank Langella in the role of Grandier.

Around the same time, the 1634 possessions inspired a film that beat Russell to the punch by ten years. In 1961, Polish director Jerzy Kawalerowicz made *Matka Joanna od*

Aniolów (*Mother Joan of the Angels*), a haunting black-and-white film that picks up where Russell's film would leave off, at Father Grandier's trial and death. *Matka Joanna od Aniolów* begins its story there, detailing the town's further possessions and the work of Father Joseph Suryn (Mieczyslaw Vojt) whose main focus is to save Sister Joan (Lucyna Winnicka), called Jeanne in Russell's film.

"It is a love story about a man and a woman who wear church clothes, and whose religion does not allow them to love each other," said Kawalerowicz. "They often talk about and teach about love — how to love God, how to love each other — and yet they cannot have the love of a man and a woman because of their religion."

In 1970 Russell told writer Gene D. Phillips he had seen Kawalerowicz's film in 1965. "My version of the story will bring in more of the political background of the period than did the Polish film," he said, adding, "My Catholic background helps me to distinguish between normal religious practices and the bizarre things attributed to the nuns in *The Devils*. Since Kawalerowicz is not a Christian, the whole idea of convent life would seem bizarre to him."

Yet another adaptation of the possessions at Loudun was taken up by a Polish artist, eight years after Kawalerowicz's film.

Superstar Polish composer Krzysztof Penderecki once said, "All I'm interested in is liberating sound beyond all tradition." The avant-garde musician whose compositions for orchestra include traditional instruments (occasionally played in novel ways) as well as typewriters and musical saws forged a reputation for creating unusual and striking symphonic pieces. In 1968 he was commissioned by the Hamburg State Opera to create an opera based on John Whiting's play.

Premiering on June 20, 1969, *The Devils of Loudun* (*Die Teufel von Loudon*), Penderecki's atonal opera in three acts, became a European hit. Since then the opera has played internationally to very mixed reviews. In 1970 a critic in West Berlin called the opera "an electrifying unforgettable experience" while a French audience responded to the show in 1972 by catcalling and pelting the stage with orange peels, turnips and leeks.

At the same time as Penderecki's contraltos and bass baritones were dodging produce on the French stage, Ken Russell was blurring the line between Huxley's book and Whiting's play, creating his own twisted version of the possessions at Loudun.

"It's easier if the director does the adaptation himself," said Russell, "or so I thought when I was commissioned to write a script for *The Devils*. Not only did I have at my disposal Aldous Huxley's masterful novel *The Devils of Loudun*, but also John Whiting's dynamic play *The Devils*. The script could hardly fail."

Russell shares a writing credit on *The Devils* with Whiting and Huxley (both of whom had shuffled off by this time) but it can't really be said that the movie is a direct adaptation of either man's work. "I also used the available documentation, but I had to thin it out since it is so vast," he said in an interview with Gene D. Phillips.

"I'd say there's about a third from the play," Russell told interviewer Terry Curtis Fox, "but some of that is superimposed over Huxley, anyway. I suppose mainly Huxley for the atmosphere. I thought the play was rather sentimental. When I first saw it in 1961 I was knocked out by it. Dorothy Tutin played Sister Jeanne and she was wonderful. Then I read it again just before I started the screenplay. It was very good dialogue, but I thought it evaded the central issue. I thought it was soft-centered; it wasn't hard enough."

Russell toughened up the story — although he is quick to say he had to downplay some of the more horrifying images in Huxley's work — but more importantly he had finally come across a story that could bear his mad, extravagant visual style. Russell praised Huxley's book for giving him the chance to take the real life events and "not only 'open them out' [filmmaker slang for expanding the settings of the play and the novel] but turn them inside out and stand them on their head."

It was the movie he had been working toward his entire career: a story whose inherent baroque decadence — and historical fact — could hold up to the director's renegade, fabulist Gothic style. Huxley's suggestion that the tortured nuns of Loudun "have been turned into cabaret performers and circus freaks" must have piqued Russell's imagination.

"*The Devils* particularly appealed to me because it was the first well-recorded witch hunt," he said. "And witch hunts come up all the time."

Murray Melvin, who plays the masturbating priest, Father Mignon, in the film, sees a parallel between Russell and the material. "I've always thought the movie summed up Ken," he told me in 2011. "When you read the actual Huxley book, it is man against the establishment. If there was ever a parallel with Ken [that's it]. I can see why he did it. It is the fight of the individual against bureaucracy and the state and ignorance."

When I asked Melvin if he thought Russell's dogged determination to get the film made was because the story struck such a personal chord with him, he said, "I'm sure. I'm sure. It just speaks Ken. And Oliver Reed, dear darling Ollie, gave such a wonderful performance [as Grandier]. But it wasn't Ollie; it was Ken!"

In 1996 Russell told film critic Mark Kermode, "When I first read the story I was knocked out by it — it was just so shocking! — and I wanted others to be knocked out by it too."

Others felt that Russell's loosened grip on his own Catholicism may have had something to do with his interest in the story. "One was assuming at the time that he was fighting his own devils with his Catholicism going down the pan," Judith Paris told me in 2011, and Oliver Reed biographer Cliff Goodwin suggested that the actor felt that "Russell turned himself into his own demigod."

"Count how many times his name appears in the titles," Reed snorted. "I suspect him a bit."

Whatever the reason, the source material certainly fed Russell's imagination. Editor Michael Bradsell remembered, "He said that when he had been asked to make a film of *The Devils* he consulted two sources, John Whiting's play and Aldous Huxley's novel, and found that he could write a script almost as fast as he could put pen to paper. It took him about three weeks and it never needed to be altered."

To remind people that what they were seeing was real and not the blasphemous ravings of a lapsed Catholic, Russell first penned the words: "This film is based on historical fact. The principal characters lived and the major events depicted in the film actually took place."

For filmgoers, Loudun and Russell would be a marriage made in heaven; for censors, hell.

"Once I had decided to do *The Devils*," Russell said, "I had to go along with the truth as it was reported. I had to show the violent atmosphere that the plague had created at the time, for instance, in order to explain how ordinary people could stand by and allow a man they knew to be innocent to die a hideous death. They had become calloused as the result of the plague. When there is death on every doorstep, the death of a man like Grandier becomes inconsequential, an everyday occurrence. That is why the crowd behaved at his burning as if they were attending a football match."

The trick was to shape that story into cinematic form. In his Sunday *Times* column on adapting books for the screen, Russell said that "when I tot up the number of feature films to my credit (or otherwise), I find that more than half of them have been adaptations of literary works" and notes that "in bringing a novel of several hundred pages to the screen something has to go."

In this case it was a balancing act of weaving together the two sources while keeping in mind the running time, or what he called the B.F. Factor — that's butt fatigue, or how long the average person will tolerate sitting in a cinema seat. *Women in Love*, for instance, has a B.F. Factor of two hours six minutes.

To hit a B.F. Factor of 111 minutes for *The Devils*, Russell squeezed the timeline of a number of events from several years to several months, and he eliminated or altered some elements, including numerous appeals, the complicated back-and-forth between the secular and ecclesiastical courts and the Father Barre story line.

He looked to Huxley's book for the tone of the film. The violence, edge and gruesome humor of Huxley's prose formed the backbone of the script, but Russell tempers several of the brutal scenes with dark humor. For example, as Grandier is being tortured before being burned at the stake Baron de Laubardemont asks, "Tell me, do you love the Church?"

"Not today," comes the reply, with timing that wouldn't have been out of place in Monty Python's *The Life of Brian*.

Another scene shows Russell's ability to meld horror and humor. In a sequence inspired by true events and detailed in Huxley's book, incompetent inquisitors Ibert, Adam and Barre examine Sister Jeanne's vomit, looking for evidence to be used against Grandier.

Barre: Tell me, tell me.

Ibert: That's a left ventricle.

Adam: It's part of the heart of a child.

Barre: Sacrificed at a witches' Sabbath, no doubt. Look! A consecrated wafer.

Adam: Yeah. Blood, thick blood. The blood of a man.

Barre: Yeah, Grandier.

Ibert: That slimy stuff could only be semen.

Barre: And what's that?

Adam: That's a carrot.

"[T]ake a phrase like 'They analyzed her vomit,'" said Russell. "It's in the book but people don't believe it or can't visualize it. The list of things in the vomit was exactly what one of the inquisitors gave — saving the carrots — and I think that, for a lot of people, the film was the first insight into what a holy interrogation in those days was really all about. The inclusion of a comic line about the carrot was typical of many deliberate ludicrous touches throughout the film, designed to point out the nonsensical irony of these horrors being committed in the name of God. The Church had her vomit analyzed but it was done, not by a surgeon as we understand them today, but by a barber and grocer. The whole film was conceived as a black comedy . . ."

A black comedy perhaps, but one that maintains the social commentary and context of Huxley's book. This is not history preserved in aspic. Russell skillfully weaves modern themes of the threat to individual rights and spiritual liberty from irrationality, social hysteria and authoritarianism throughout, echoing Huxley.

Most importantly, as author Joseph Gomez notes in *Ken Russell*, the director wrote a script that "is about a past which warns us about the present and possible future. As such the anachronisms begin a filmic working out of

Huxley's numerous references to twentieth-century life — a visual embodiment of perhaps the most crucial aspect of Huxley's *The Devils of Loudun.*"

From Whiting, Russell lifts some dialogue and the playwright's technique of juxtaposing scenes to compress the narrative. For example, Russell intercuts between a wild orgiastic dance of the nuns and an introspective scene of Father Grandier holding a simple mass for himself on a riverbank.

A major change occurred once the first rough draft of the script had been completed. In Russell's first version of the script, Sister Jeanne was the major focus of the story, not Grandier. Originally Russell wanted to show what happened to the sister and Richelieu but he was stymied by the B.F. Factor. "Because the script was too long, we had to cut out all [the] material which tended to make Jeanne the focus of the story," said Russell.

"At the end de Laubardemont says, 'You're stuck in this convent for life,' but as soon as he'd gone Jeanne set about getting out, because her brief moment of notoriety had whetted her appetite for more. So she gouged a couple of holes in her hands and pretended she had stigmata, saw 'visions' and, with the help of Sister Agnes, gulled some old priest into thinking she was the greatest lady since Virgin Mary. So she and Agnes went on a jaunt all over France and were hailed with as much fervor as showbiz personalities and pop stars are received today. In Paris, 30,000 people assembled outside her hotel in the hope of getting a glimpse of her. She became very friendly with Richelieu, the king and queen wined and dined her and she had a grand old time."

But instead, Russell focused on Grandier, a character the director said "represents the paradox of the Catholic Church." It's clear that Russell, who converted to Catholicism — or became, as he says, "a Catholic space cadet" — in 1957, allowed his religion to seep into virtually all his movies. In a *Sunday Times* piece the director cited his greatest influences. Coming in at number eight, several steps below Busby Berkeley and classical music, was "one of my greatest influences of all — the Catholic Church."

"When I was young, I didn't really know where I was going," Russell said, "but as soon as I came into the faith, my work, my philosophy, gained direction. Except for *The Boy Friend* — a pathetic event — all my films have been Catholic films, films about love, faith, sin, guilt, forgiveness, redemption. Films that could only have been made by a Catholic."

Religious symbols and themes are peppered throughout his films. Russell scholar Iain Fisher wrote, "There are three overlapping phases [to Russell's career]: the devout Catholic, the Catholic testing faith to its limits and the irreverence of later years as organized religion fails to live up to expectations."

One of Russell's early mentors, the BBC's Sir Huw Wheldon — whose motto "make the good popular, and the popular good" was the director's mantra during his time at Monitor — once admonished the filmmaker "in a voice that still echoes," as he was about to start his drama-documentary on the Roman Catholic composer Elgar: "Not too many bloody crucifixes now, Russell."

Later works like *Tommy* have fun with Catholic iconography, for instance changing a blind, deaf and dumb pinball wizard into a messiah who can literally walk on water. *Lisztomania* also plays up the place of religion in popular culture, showing Ringo Starr as the pope, and rock stars Elvis Presley and Pete Townshend as icons.

The idea of the "whisky priest" pops up in *Crimes of Passion* and *Lion's Mouth* among others; images of Christ and crucifixions appear in everything from *Amelia and the*

Angel, *Elgar*, *Lisztomania* and *Tommy* to later films like *Lair of the White Worm* and *Gothic*; and Russell even played a fornicating priest in *Song of Summer*. But *The Devils* is the pinnacle of his skeptical look at the Church. "The film has some things to say about the Church," he said, "but the Church will survive it."

The Devils, Russell went on to explain, is a Christian film about a sinner who becomes a saint. The main appeal for Russell was his new main character, Grandier, a man not unlike the protagonists of his last two films — Gerald from *Women in Love* and Tchaikovsky from *The Music Lovers*. They are all men who aspired to a more patrician place in life.

"Grandier is a mixture of good and bad qualities," Russell said. "He knows what he should do, but he often doesn't do it, as Saint Paul once said. Then he gets the opportunity to stand up against Richelieu in order to pre- serve the rights of the city and he does so. In this crisis his good qualities come to the surface and he dies a Christian martyr for his people."

He also saw parallels with other historical figures: "[Grandier was] like many of my heroic characters . . . great despite himself. Most of the people in my films are taken a bit by surprise, like Isadora Duncan and Delius. They're out of step with their times and their society, but nevertheless manage to produce rather extraordinary changes in atti- tudes and events. This was exactly Grandier's situation. He was a minor priest who was used as a fall guy in a political conflict, who lost his life and his battle but won the war.

"We know from history that the State usually survives while the individual loses out in these cases; but I wanted to examine what lasting impact the individual still has, even when he loses."

† ‡ †

Script in place, Russell was ready to begin preproduction. Or was he? There were still a couple of hurdles, one that proved almost insurmountable.

As a matter of course, in 1969, Russell ran the script past John Trevelyan, secretary of the British Board of Film Censors (BBFC). Trevelyan looked as one might image a censor: thick glasses fronted a schoolmaster's face. While he was rarely seen in anything but a starched white shirt under a nondescript black suit, he brought a liberal slant to the BBFC during its most tumultuous decade — the 1960s.

Established in 1912, the British Board of Film Censors was an industry watchdog that rated and regulated the nation's film business. Notable rulings included cutting *Rebel Without a Cause* in order to quell the "possibility of teenage rebellion" and outright banning *The Texas Chainsaw Massacre* and *Last House on the Left*. In 1984 the organization replaced the word "censor" in its name with "classification" to "reflect the fact that classification plays a far larger part in the Board's work than censorship."

Progressive isn't usually a word associated with censors but Trevelyan was just that, ushering in an era of unprecedented violence, drug use, strong language, frontal nudity and graphic sex scenes on British screens. Before his era, the BBFC had been eager to protect the gentle sensibilities of the British public, even barring "abdominal contortions in dancing."

"We are paid to have dirty minds," he famously said, and during his tenure — certainly the BBFC's palmiest days — he made sure the censor's office stayed abreast of social change and the public's rapidly changing pulse. Judging a film's content on its context and artistic merit became key factors when determining the rating a movie received. This sea change in attitude won him the gratitude of many film-makers, but not all. His fierce criticism of the violence in the early Bond films won him a dubious tribute: in 1995's James Bond flick *Goldeneye* the villain is named Alec Trevelyan.

Broad-minded as he was, the script for *The Devils* presented some problems and after thoroughly studying the script he sent Russell a detailed letter containing numerous scenes he felt would need to be cut or altered.

A bigger concern was the reaction of United Artists, who had commissioned the script. Even though Russell had already directed three movies for them (*Billion Dollar Brain*, 1967; *Women in Love*, 1969; *The Music Lovers*, 1970), *The Devils* was promptly dropped when "somebody at UA actually read the script." Unable to come to terms, UA and Russell went their separate ways, even though months of work had already gone into the script and preproduction.

At the time Russell was editing *The Music Lovers*, he told journalist Gene D. Phillips, "I don't mind now if I am not able to make [*The Devils*] since I have worked it out shot by shot in my imagination; I can run it in my head any time I want to. Although I must admit a finished film is often very different from the way one has initially pictured it in one's mind."

Despite his bluster, United Artists' change of heart was seen as a setback and not the death of the project.

"After United Artists pulled out of *The Devils*," said Russell, "we were out on a limb. Derek Jarman had done designs for the film. I'd written the script, Shirley [Russell, his wife] had designed the costumes. It would have been a disaster to scrap all that work. Bob Solo, the producer who had spent years getting the rights to Huxley's book and the Whiting play, started looking around for another backer, but it took about four months of offering the package to various companies before Warner Brothers agreed to have a go."

Chapter Three

CASTING *THE DEVILS*

"What fresh lunacy is this?" — Grandier

As any director knows, casting a film is ninety percent of the job. To fill the two lead roles of Grandier and Sister Jeanne, Russell set his sights on two actors he not only had experience with, but knew would be perfect for the parts. Imagining a return to the success of *Women in Love* he wanted to reunite that film's two biggest stars, Oliver Reed and Glenda Jackson.

Grandier, the philandering whisky priest, was a role Oliver Reed was born to play. The character's pursuit of physical pleasure echoed the actor's own hedonistic penchant for drinking and womanizing, and Grandier's sense of place — his loyalty to Loudun — mirrored Reed's commitment to Old Blighty. Both are complex, deeply flawed men whose appetites overshadowed their accomplishments. In the film Grandier says, "I have loved women and enjoyed power, but I shall never be the Devil's boy . . . I haven't got the humility," a quote that could have easily come from the loquacious actor rather than his character.

"[Grandier] is a man who is loved by women," says critic Nigel Floyd in the documentary *Hell on Earth*. "He is a man who's loved women. Women would say about him, 'Now there's a man worth going to hell for.'"

Reed had big shoes to fill but his flamboyant swagger and charisma more than make Grandier believable as a character. To paraphrase Raymond Chandler, Grandier was a man who could make a nun kick a hole in a stained glass window, and Reed pulls it off.

Writer Jim Emerson described Reed's Grandier as "a shaggy-haired, mustached priest who looks like he just came from a Doobie Brothers concert (singing 'Jesus Is Just Alright,' no doubt)," but Reed brings a messianic air to the role, a crucial trait for Russell's Christ allegory. Not only do we see Grandier walking on water in one of Sister Jeanne's visions, but he is killed by his own people for refusing to go against his principles, just like the Christ he worships.

"The character of the priest was a marvelous one to act," said Reed after shooting was complete. "Ken Russell's brother-in-law is an historian and he helped me research Grandier's life, with particular reference to his thesis in celibacy. The people of Loudun loved him. He walked among the plague victims and comforted them. I started to play him as a priest and realized that he was a politician."

"Oliver Reed, who had such a terrible reputation, was really, really nice to me," said Gemma Jones, who played Madeleine de Brou, Grandier's mistress and later wife. "I knew all about [his fierce reputation] but he was very considerate and very helpful and behaved impeccably on set, in my memory. What he got up to off the set, one heard about but he was hugely professional on set. I think he knew I was very young, green and innocent and he was very helpful."

"He had tremendous, tremendous energy," remembered co-star Dudley Sutton, who made three films with Reed. "He'd be out on the razzle all night, virtually, have about an hour's sleep, come on the set and — I did this once with him in Hungary — charge around, galloping a horse around the place and do a massive amount of sword fighting. He just had tremendous energy and one had the feeling in those days that one day he'd pop, which is indeed what he did."

Mark Strong, the handsome English star of *Body of Lies* and *Robin Hood* for director Ridley Scott, told me what Scott said about working with Reed. "He said to Ridley, 'In the week I'm yours, in the weekend I'm on my own.' That was the deal and Ollie stuck to that. In fact, I think he died on the weekend and finished his pint before he went." (Reed died of a heart attack during a break from filming Scott's *Gladiator* in Valletta, Malta, on May 2, 1999, after a night of heavy drinking and arm wrestling with off-duty sailors.)

Casting Sister Jeanne, the erotomanic hunchbacked nun, proved more difficult. The role was originally offered to Glenda Jackson, an actress Russell called "impeccable." They had history — she had won an Academy Award for her work with Russell in *Women in Love* and starred as Tchaikovsky's vulnerable, unloved wife Nina in *The Music Lovers* — but she backed out when her role was modified.

In Russell's original script Sister Jeanne was the central character whose story carried on after Grandier was burned at the stake. The version Jackson agreed to do included several showy scenes displaying Jeanne's unquenchable thirst for attention. Unfortunately, because of the script's length, Russell had to slash many of those scenes, including her self-inflicted stigmata sequence, her wining and dining with the king and queen of France, her near-rock-star status — thousands of people mobbed her hotel to catch a glimpse of her — and her enshrinement when her decapitated head was placed on display at her convent.

"We had to cut out all this material which tended to make Sister Jeanne the focus of the story," said Russell, "and I think this is why Glenda Jackson eventually refused the part. When she saw the final script which ended with Grandier's death, she said, 'This is not the way you told it to me,' which I had to admit was true. She'd loved the idea of her head in a casket and everyone worshipping her on their knees. And with all that gone she'd have been just back in the madhouse again."

It has also been suggested that it wasn't so much the size

of the role that led Jackson to decline, but that the idea of playing another sexually fixated lead in a Ken Russell movie didn't appeal to her. Forty years later Jackson confirmed this to me. In an email exchange, Mrs. Rebecca Henney, Senior Parliamentary Assistant to Glenda Jackson MP, wrote, "Glenda has asked me to respond to your email about Ken Russell's film, *The Devils*. Quite simply she did not wish to play another neurotic."

"Ken wanted me to be in this film *The Devils*," she said in a 1971 *New York Times* interview, "but I was worried about playing another neurotic, sex-starved lady, albeit a nun. Ken is a very complex man and I think he was personally hurt when I told him I didn't want to do the film. If it still stings him, I guess that's the way it has to be."

Stung indeed. Russell told film critic and television host Rex Reed in 1971, "I'm glad she wasn't in it. She's not a very good actress; she's very cold and intellectual. No emotion. She says she doesn't want to play the same parts, yet she did Queen Elizabeth on TV like a boring schoolmistress and followed it up with a movie playing the same part. Giving a ghastly performance from what I hear." Either way she was out, and Russell had to keep looking for someone charismatic enough — and brave enough — to play the tormented Ursuline nun Huxley described as the "supernatural equivalent of a movie star." (Russell softened his feelings about Jackson's defection from the project in later years. In a piece in the *Times* he wrote that even though she declined the role "her heart is there — her relentless love of the truth.")

Jackson's replacement was an award-winning actress from one of the most storied families of the British stage. Vanessa Redgrave, the daughter of actors Sir Michael Redgrave and Rachel Kempson, and sister to acclaimed actors Lynn Redgrave and Corin Redgrave, was well known almost from the moment she was born. On January 30,

1937, Laurence Olivier announced her arrival to the audience from the stage of London's Old Vic Theatre after a performance of *Hamlet*. At the curtain he said, "Ladies and gentlemen, tonight a great actress has been born. Laertes [played by Sir Michael] has a daughter!"

She quickly got into the family business, first appearing in the West End in 1958, playing opposite her brother, when she was just twenty-one years old. By the time *The Devils* came around she was already an accomplished stage actress and film star, known for her portrayal of a hip London swinger in 1966's *Blow-Up* and as an Academy Award–nominated actress, first for *Morgan: A Suitable Case for Treatment* — which pitted her against her sister, Lynn, nominated that year for *Georgy Girl* — and for a second time for the lead in *Isadora*, a Karel Reisz–directed biopic about dancer Isadora Duncan.

Just as she was earning praise for acting — both Arthur Miller and Tennessee Williams called her "the greatest living actress of our times" — she was also gaining notoriety for her support of political causes. From opposition to the Vietnam War to nuclear disarmament, and later, the unification of Ireland and defense of the Provisional IRA, her name had frequently been a flashpoint for controversy.

Perhaps that's why she and the rabble-rousing Russell got on so well.

Both of Russell's choices for Sister Jeanne were inspired. The role requires complete dedication from the actress, a physical part that requires a lack of inhibition — one critic described it as "roaring, creaking madness." Jackson's more controlled approach might have made *The Devils* a rather different film, but Redgrave's wild abandon adds much to the final product. "Vanessa was always an adventurous type of person," said co-star Dudley Sutton.

"There are two impeccable actresses I've actually had the

privilege of working with," said Russell, changing his tune from the infamous Rex Reed interview, "Glenda Jackson and Vanessa Redgrave. There simply was no end to their genius. Whatever character they were playing, they absorbed it totally. Glenda oozed power and self-possession in *Women in Love*, woundedness and need in *The Music Lovers*. One would never guess that seconds before a challenging scene as a murderous queen [in *Salome's Last Dance*] she would 'prepare' by listening to Women's Hour on the radio in her dressing room.

"Or that Vanessa would complete a scripted nervous breakdown on-screen as the schizophrenic nun in *The Devils*, then rush out to sell *The Daily Worker* at the studio gates. At the sound of the clapperboard these big stars were as focused as astronauts on the way to achieving lift-off — as luminous as angels, as nuanced as smoke, as riveting as tornadoes. How they managed it is known only to themselves, as I was too discreet ever to pry."

Co-star Gemma Jones, who plays Grandier's bride Madeleine de Brou, shared some very powerful scenes with Vanessa Redgrave but her initial meeting with the star was inauspicious. "I came into the makeup caravan and I hadn't met [Vanessa Redgrave] before and I stood behind her as she was being made up and said hello, and she was rather cool. She wasn't very friendly. It didn't worry me particularly.

"I sat down to have my makeup done and she stood up from her chair. She's terribly tall so that startled me a bit. She stood up and seemed to go on forever. Then she bent right down onto the makeup table and felt on the makeup table for her glasses, and I realized that she was so short-sighted and when she wasn't wearing her contact lenses, that she didn't know who was standing behind her, saying hello.

"It wasn't that she was being unfriendly; she just couldn't see me. That always made her very intense, even on the stage because sometimes she couldn't see people from one side of the stage to the other. But she was very nice to me."

The rest of the cast were a blend of Ken Russell's Informal Repertory Company — such as Russell regular Graham Armitage, who appeared in both *The Music Lovers* and *The Boy Friend* and played Louis XIII in *The Devils* — and well-cast character actors.

As Sister Agnes, a spy planted in the convent by Cardinal Richelieu, Russell cast Judith Paris. In the credits she is listed erroneously as Sister Judith, a mistake Paris chalks up to the fact that her part was reduced in the editing room. "I looked at the credits the other day and I thought, 'My God, I'm down as Sister Judith.' Agnes was Richelieu's niece and originally had a large speaking role, but most of her dialogue ended up on the cutting room floor.

"She was a plant," said Paris. "Richelieu just wanted the dirt on Sister Jeanne and what Sister Agnes found out was that Sister Jeanne was quite frankly mad."

The Royal Ballet School student and dancer had worked extensively with the director on his BBC bio-pics, including *Dance of the Seven Veils* and *Dante's Inferno* (opposite Oliver Reed).

"I adored Ken," she said. "I absolutely adored him and I was so proud to be a part of his ensemble as it were. He persuaded me to chuck the dancing and to start acting. I had known him for a number of years before I did *The Devils* and I had always thought of him as being the most special and unique and extraordinary person."

In the key role of Father Barre, Russell cast Michael Gothard — "looking for all the world," wrote *Photoplay Monthly*, "like Mick Jagger in the wrong century" — an English character actor best remembered for his role as Kai in the television series *Arthur of the Britons* and as the mysterious, nonspeaking villain Emile Leopold Locque in the

1981 James Bond film *For Your Eyes Only*. Two years after he burned Reed to a crisp in *The Devils*, he reteamed with Reed in *The Three Musketeers* and *The Four Musketeers* (both films were shot simultaneously) as assassin John Felton.

The role of the Machiavellian Baron de Laubardemont — the man who is rebuffed by Grandier when he arrives with orders to destroy Loudun, and then summons "professional witch-hunter" Father Pierre Barre — was a pivotal one.

A distant relative of Sister Jeanne des Anges and a key figure in Richelieu's campaign of eliminating Huguenot influence by destroying local strongholds, de Laubardemont was sent to Loudun to oversee the tearing down of the town's fortifications, but when stymied by Grandier he helped fabricate a case against him, coercing false statements of demonic possession from Sister Jeanne and the Ursuline nuns. Through his efforts, Grandier was executed and Loudun's walls were torn down, further strengthening de Laubardemont's boss Cardinal Richelieu's power within the church and France.

De Laubardemont was played by Dudley Sutton, an eccentric English actor who became a cult figure after playing a gay biker in 1964's *The Leather Boys*. "I would not have gotten near that film if a lot of people hadn't turned it down," he told me in 2011. "The respectable actors turned it down. A lot of them thought it was blasphemous, which it is not. I've always found that when people accuse something of being blasphemous it's always, invariably, not. It's just a fresh and open approach.

"I wasn't very well known at the time, but [Russell] did like people who came from the theater where Murray [Melvin] and I had come from, Joan Littlewood's Theatre Workshop. We were known to be adventurous and we were known to be very good at ad-libbing. We were known to be much more adaptable than the standard English actors of the time. We were also better trained in the sense that we were good at dance and movement rather than the actors in those days who just weren't . . . they were very rigid. In that sense it was understandable that he would have auditioned me for it."

To clinch the gig Sutton lied to Russell, telling him he was able to ride a horse for his dramatic entrance in the film. "In the course of the interview he said, 'Can you ride?' and I said yes," Sutton told me. "I could just about get on a horse, although I hadn't done so since I was very young. When it came time to shoot, it was obvious I wasn't a very good horseman and he said, 'I thought you told me you could ride!' I said, 'Well, you wouldn't have given me the job if I said no.' 'Fucking right,' he said and walloped the horse. It went charging down the hill with me on it, looking like a sack of potatoes."

Max Adrian was cast as inquisitor Ibert, in his second to last filmed performance (his final work came in Russell's next film *The Boy Friend*) of a thirty-five-year film career. He had appeared in the stage version of *The Devils* ten years before Russell brought it to the screen.

Rounding out the main cast was oddball actor Murray Melvin — best known for having created the role of Geoffrey in the stage and film versions of *A Taste of Honey*. He was cast as the elderly masturbating priest Mignon, even though he was only thirty-eight years old at the time.

"I was sent the script [with a note] saying, 'Look at Mignon. I want you to do Mignon,'" said Melvin. "So I raced to a bookshop to get the Huxley to do my home-work, and as I'm reading my heart was sinking because I was reading that Father Mignon was sort of a doddering old eighty-five-year-old and I'm thinking, 'Oh no. I'm not right.

Oh how sad, all this wonderful story.'

"The next week I was going to [Russell's] home to talk about it and I got there and he poured me a glass and we were having a nice quiet drink and he said, 'What do you think?'

"I said, 'Ken, it is the most wonderful story but I'm terribly worried. I don't want you to make a mistake. Father Mignon is eighty-five years old.' Of course I was almost fifty years younger.

"He looked at me with disgust and said, 'Of course I know he's an eighty-five-year-old. But you can do something with it, can't you?'

"'Oh yes, Ken, I can do something with it,' I said. 'Thank you. Fill that glass up again.'"

Such is the mystery of Russell's casting technique. He didn't usually do auditions — Gemma Jones told me she didn't remember an audition, and when asked if there was an audition process for *The Devils*, Melvin said, "Oh good Lord no, not with Ken." — but relied on his instincts.

"Ken is very astute," said Melvin, noting that he has no idea why the director cast him as Mignon. "I don't know because I hadn't done that kind of evil character for him before. I'd worked with him when he was working for the BBC on the *Monitor* program. My first thing I did for him was George Grossmith's *Diary of a Nobody* [playing Lupin Pooter], which I am proud to say is also banned. I said to him on Sunday, 'It would be a good epitaph; I was in Ken Russell films that are banned.' That'll sort you out from the crowd. And that was a comedic part as a dancer and comedic. Then I did a tiny little part for him at the end of *Isadora* and the next bit was *The Devils*."

He continued by saying, "I'm eternally grateful to him. May I say that the lovely thing from an actor's point of view with Ken, why one adores him so much apart from the person itself, is that as a director he gave you different parts. Very often you work for directors who cast you in the same mold, but not Ken. He was forever giving us totally different parts."

As Cardinal Richelieu, Russell cast colorful English poet Christopher Logue. Logue was an interesting choice to play the vengeful Richelieu. A literary jack-of-all-trades, he spent forty-five years reworking *The Iliad* and who would later write the screenplay for *Savage Messiah*, Russell's acclaimed look at the life of French sculptor Henri Gaudier-Brzeska. Logue's only other high-profile film role was as the "spaghetti-eating fanatic" in Terry Gilliam's *Jabberwocky* (1977), but as a writer he won the Whitbread Poetry Prize in 2005 and was awarded the C.B.E. (Commander of the Order of the British Empire) in 2007. "I needed a bit of change to keep my interest going," he later said of his varied and eclectic career.

Years before he played Admiral Piett in *The Empire Strikes Back* and *Return of the Jedi*, Kenneth Colley was cast as Legrand. Colley was a stock member of Russell's crew, making appearances in his films over a two-decade period. He played Modeste in *The Music Lovers*, Chopin in *Lisztomania*, Dreyfus in *Prisoners of Honor* and had roles in *Mahler*, *The Rainbow* and *Arnold Bax*. The actor was known to have a stutter in real life, but when he had a role in a film could say his lines without a trace of a stammer.

As Philippe, the young woman Grandier impregnates, Russell cast television actress Georgina Hale. "She [is] the one that put the finger on Grandier when he throws her over, the one who really starts the ball rolling," said Russell. "I first met [Georgina] when we were casting for *Women in Love* and I thought she looked interesting. Then we did another casting session for *The Devils*. She came into my office, sat down and something seemed to exude from her which was very sensual and powerful. She seemed terribly self-assured and funny. I like working with people who have a sense of humor. They've got to have a sense of humor to be in my films." In 1975 Hale would win a BAFTA Film Award for Most Promising Newcomer to Leading Film Roles for Ken Russell's *Mahler*.

Looking back at the film forty years later, *Toxic Avenger* director Lloyd Kaufman praised the cast. "How great that these major stars like Oliver Reed and Vanessa Redgrave and others in the movie took it all the way," he said. "They had no fear. They were risking their careers. Nineteen seventy-one, it was only a few years since the blacklisting and people were getting arrested and being put in jail for porno. In the United States there were scenes in there that could have been accused of transporting obscenity across state lines. I don't think George Clooney or Adam Sandler would do anything that risky, and that adventuresome. You definitely don't have that kind of bravery today."

Chapter Four

SIGHTS AND SOUNDS OF *THE DEVILS*

"Look at your city! If your city is destroyed,
your freedom is destroyed also."
— Father Grandier

Michael Derek Elworthy Jarman's Wikipedia entry lists him as "an English film director, stage designer, diarist, artist, gardener and author." He was certainly all those things and more in his all-too-short life (he died in 1994 at age fifty-four from AIDS-related complications), but when Ken Russell first encountered him he was a burgeoning artist with just a handful of credits to his name.

"A lot of things in my life are by accident or chance," said Russell. "A friend of my wife's was a dress designer, and she said one day, 'Oh, I just came back from Paris and I met someone interesting on the train; I think you should meet him.' I said 'Who's that?' and she said, 'His name is Derek Jarman. And he actually got up and gave me his seat and we got talking and the train was packed. He had a folder of his work and I had a folder of my work and we showed it to each other and he is innovative and has got lots of ideas, and you are looking for a designer for *The Devils*, aren't you?' and I said, 'Yes I am.' And she said, 'You could do worse than look at him.'

"So I sought him out and he was living in a vast room in a deserted storage place [at 13 Bankside near the Cannon Street Tube in London]. And in the middle of it he had erected a small greenhouse which he could heat, because he couldn't heat this vast room, which was freezing. It was the middle of winter. So there he was in this glass house and I went in and said hello. He had an exhibition he was getting ready for called Cardinal's Capes. I can't remember them all, but there was one [cape] made of dollar bills and there was a transparent one of a junky found below his river, his warehouse; that's where he lived in a warehouse and stuff like that. We talked a bit and I thought this has to be the guy, he's an iconoclast, he knows about religion, he has feelings and his mind is wide open. It was not cluttered with any preconceived thing. He had never done a film before, he had designed a ballet I think, or two, or maybe an opera. But I could see he was a real talent."

Jarman remembers the meeting, the freezing cold room and the mugs of tea they used to warm themselves as he showed the director "odd drawings from *Jazz Calendar* and *The Don*, plus various other projects I had worked on. After looking at them briefly he asked me to design *The Devils*. I was quite taken aback by the suddenness of this offer . . ."

Looking around the room at the unusually decorated cardinals' capes, Russell was immediately struck by the young artist's interesting take on organized religion. He liked how Jarman's sarcasm and irreverence contrasted and complemented his own deeply felt Catholic beliefs. By this point in his life, more than a decade after his conversion to Catholicism, Russell had, as one writer put it, "created his own version of the faith, stronger on mysticism and superstition than philosophy."

As the patron saint of iconoclasts, Russell practiced his faith in a manner almost as strange as Jarman's physical manifestations of it. Example? Russell claimed to have beaten his addiction to snuff by praying to a Virgin Mary statue while riding on top of a London bus.

"I thought at once," Russell told *Sight & Sound*, "this was the guy for me."

Jarman was initially reluctant. After designing *Through-way* for Ballet Rambert (a show so critically savaged that choreographer Steve Popescu committed suicide afterward) and a disastrous experience designing John Gielgud's English National Opera production of *Don Giovanni* for the stage, he had vowed never to design again. Russell gave him just twenty-four hours to decide, time Jarman used well. "In the evening I rushed out to see *Women in Love*," Jarman wrote in his memoir *Dancing Ledge*. "On the strength of that, and conversations with a few friends, I decided to plunge in."

Their collaboration proved to be a turning point for Jarman even though he would later say, "I learnt how not to make films from Ken Russell, and how to make them from Kenneth Anger." The experience of designing *The Devils* opened up a new world for the artist, who immediately started dabbling with a Super 8 camera before focusing on film as a career.

"He was one of the most interesting people I ever met," said Russell in *Sight & Sound*. "He was very keen to do the film. We talked and talked for days on end. Even if I didn't always use his ideas, they invariably sparked off other ideas. I remember he wanted a dream sequence with Sister Jeanne burdened down with thousands of crucifixes and crawling through a desert of martyrs hanging from trees."

Russell, who had made many period pieces for both small and large screens, had a different vision for *The Devils*. As befits a man who once proclaimed, "I'm eaten up with the image, with the way things look!" Russell had very definite ideas on the design for *The Devils*. Pulling inspiration from Huxley's book, he wanted to make a historical film with a progressive look and feel.

"I was sick of historical films which were approached in a very clichéd way," he said in 1975. "I went to the Pinewood studios and I said, 'We will need to build a tower.' And they said, 'We've got molds for building you seventeenth-century walls.' They took me to see these old molds and they were in the shape of crumbling walls. I said, 'Well, yeah . . . but they wouldn't have been crumbling when they were built.'

"That never seemed to have struck anybody. It came as a great revelation to them that they didn't actually build crumbling stone. I said, 'We need to make it feel as though it wasn't an old crumbling city to them. To them, it was a modern city.'"

"I wanted to get a feeling of this happening to a set of people who consider themselves modern," he said in a separate interview. "I'm sure to every person at every stage in history their town has not been an old-fashioned town, their town has been a modern town and they are modern people."

To this end he and Jarman chose not to slavishly replicate the clichéd architectural look of seventeenth-century France, but instead create futuristic sets that thematically suggest historical France. It's a tactic Jarman employed again in his rebellious, anachronistic designs for his historical films, *Caravaggio* (1986) and *Edward II* (1991).

"He does incredibly well at portraying a period that is eminently modern with the sets and the wardrobe design," said Guillermo del Toro, director of *Pan's Labyrinth*, of the look and feel of Russell's film. "It feels authentic even if it is completely fake. There are acrylic doors and stainless steel surfaces and [Father Barre] looks like John Lennon. But it feels like that is how it must have felt to live back then. It's fantastic."

An American Werewolf in London director John Landis had an opposite response, telling me, "You know what drove me crazy in that film? The glasses the one monk wore . . . these wire-framed glasses which are completely anachronistic and completely wrong. I remember when I saw the film I was twenty-one, the year I made *Schlock*. When I saw the film I was very taken with it, but two things bothered me. One was that rubber hump that was so fake and the other was those glasses. Stupid things like that would take me out of the picture."

Russell and Jarman isolated a line from Huxley's book as their starting point. In the book the hunchbacked Sister Jeanne undergoes an exorcism that was, in the author's words, "tantamount to a rape in a public lavatory." It was an image Russell says was "burnt to mind."

Jarman brought this phrase to life in his epic design for the town of Loudun by incorporating white tile into the design. Reminiscent of the kind of industrial tile used in public facilities, the tile covers much of the set. The walls of the city are pristine white, and there is a stark white-tile altar in the convent's church, the site of Sister Jeanne's invasive "exorcism." Add to the glistening tile an echo of the design from one of Russell's favorite movies, Fritz Lang's *Metropolis*. Just as the beautiful design of that film is an abstraction of German society and urban condition, Jarman's designs for *The Devils* would be both a reflection of French society and an abstraction. "I want the sets to be as big as possible," Jarman wrote in his journal, "and as forceful as the sets from an old silent."

"I remember *Metropolis* with those curved archways and I thought let's go for that," said Russell, "so I and he did all the exterior things. You know it had a new look because medieval cities always were moss covered with crumbling stone but they couldn't have been like that once. They must have been bright shining bricks and that's how the people of Loudun thought of their city anyway, as a shining monument to their individuality, so it all fell into place."

In the finished film Russell uses static shots to provide an eyeful of Jarman's pristine tiled vision of the town square. The clean veneer of the city evokes a modern feel that is anachronistic in terms of the time and place but later serves as a giant, expressionistic arena for the action. These are the most impressive sets Russell ever worked on, and he uses them effectively to set the film's dramatic tone. The Gothic architecture, wrought-iron gates and giant symmetrical cathedrals add much to the film. The severe setting of *The Devils* permeates every scene, setting it apart from the garish pre-Revolutionary France of Louis XII. The wild abandon of the king is noticeably missing here, replaced by stark white tiles. This is a serious place, an ivory tower where there is no place to hide.

Rounding out a trio of inspirations were eighteenth-century Italian artist Giovanni Battista Piranesi's *Carceri d'invenzione* or *Imaginary Prisons* etchings. The prison series depicts an imaginary, spatially impossible penal complex with no beginning or end. These pictures were described by Thomas de Quincey in *Confessions of an English Opium-Eater* (1821) as "representing vast Gothic halls, on the floor of which stood all sorts of engines and machinery, wheels, cables, pulleys, levers, catapults, etc., etc., expressive of enormous power put forth, and resistance overcome," and were said to have been conceived by the artist when he was suffering from a strong fever.

The collection of fourteen drawings inspired elements of Edgar Allan Poe's "The Pit and the Pendulum," the famous library scenes in the film version of Umberto Eco's *The Name of the Rose* (1986) and even the artwork in the video game *Counter-Strike: Source*. Jarman was struck by the epic scale of the drawings and, so inspired, designed the largest sets ever used by Russell, to be built from scratch.

"The town of Loudun," said Jarman of the design process, "is an enormous task," made easier by his background in architecture and years spent studying with Sir Nikolaus Pevsner, a scholar of art history with a specialty in architecture.

Jarman worked for three months on the drawings, sketching out his ideas in sepia ink, making "meticulous drawings of the sets, stone by stone." Art director George Lack formalized them into, according to Jarman, "proper plans and elevations." From those detailed renderings art school students built a scale model of the exterior.

In May 1970, Jarman got his first lesson in the harsh realities of the film business. At a meeting with the film's American investors and Russell, Jarman watched as the "gang of Hollywood mafia" carved up his sets. "[They] took the model of Loudun up to the lot where it was dismembered with a breadknife while they argued about its size," he wrote in his journalistic memoir *Dancing Ledge*. "They posted studio assistants to mark the limits on the ground. They spent half an hour dissecting three months' work, and at one point attempted to jettison the cathedral. The set is apparently going to be the largest since the ill-fated *Cleopatra*.

"Later, Ken called to say he'd been battling with them all day. Although he'd saved Loudun, we've lost the sets for Louis XIII's palace, except for the theater and perhaps the library; so the original design will never be realized — a historical film shot entirely on sets."

It wouldn't be the only time Jarman's *Devils* sets were mistreated. After painstakingly recreating scads of Renaissance-era art — including an elaborate facsimile of Nicolas Poussin's painting *The Triumph of Pan* — he had to stand by and watch his work be destroyed. "When I built the room," Jarman said, "I had no foreknowledge that Ken Russell was going to have it smashed to pieces in the scene in which Grandier is led to his death. I stood looking on with complete horror as this destruction was completed, carrying with it even the Poussin." (Incidentally, *The Triumph of Pan* Derek Jarman recreated and hung in Grandier's apartment is an anachronism. The painting, depicting a pagan cele-bration, was commissioned by Cardinal de Richelieu and therefore unlikely to be in Grandier's possession, and it was not completed until 1636, two years after the priest was burned at the stake.)

In the end Jarman found a way to make the budgetary cuts work in his favor. He simplified the set, stripping away the costly design frills, giving the city wall set a severe, mod-ernist look that suited the harsh story being told in front of it. Its sterile, clean look — it was constructed of beige brick that registered as white on film — was truly evocative of Huxley's "rape in a public lavatory" description.

The immense set was built at a cost of £97,000 (roughly £1,020,000 in 2011 pounds sterling) in August 1970 at Pinewood Studios, located twenty miles west of central London. The legendary film studio has been in constant operation since 1934, and has hosted literally thousands of film shoots — including *Black Narcissus*, the *Carry On* movies, most of the James Bond films, *The Shining*, *Star Wars* and the two parts of *Harry Potter and the Deathly Hallows* — and television productions.

Stephen Pickard, who spent six years as the studio's pro-jectionist, remembered seeing the completed set. "Pinewood had extensive grounds at the rear of the studio," he said, "known as the back lot, where all the exterior sets are con-structed. The most memorable sets that I recall were the city of Loudun. This was a massive set that had a large cathedral at one end and a wall and other small buildings constructed in a circular fashion all in white."

During production, however, he stayed away. "*The Devils* was one production that closed the stages to outsiders, includ-ing myself, as there was a lot of nudity involved. I recall that the Pinewood management weren't too happy with what was rumored to be going on behind locked doors!"

Although modified from the original plan, the finished sets were impressive and almost overwhelming to the actors and crew. "It was the best British design this century, I should think," said sculptor Christopher Hobbs, "amazing stuff."

"The art direction by Derek Jarman is absolutely sublime. He has such a stark, operatic, theatrical sense of set design with the white walls and the black-and-white nuns," said Guillermo del Toro. "It is just aesthetically perfect while provocatively political and incredibly shocking."

"It was astounding," said Murray Melvin. "You had to watch for your footprints! You couldn't get any dirt on the bottom of your shoes. That set remained pristine throughout the whole of the twelve weeks shooting. There was an awful lot of cleaning going on every night. But it was startling, wasn't it?"

"One can't help but be very conscious that one was walking into something extremely beautiful," said Oliver Reed. "It was very impressive and immediately moving; marvelous cathedrals and houses and people, all handpicked by Ken Russell for their fantastic character faces."

Despite being in awe of his sets, Russell didn't spare Jarman if the director was unhappy with a scene. After Jarman innocently made a change to the design of the town, he felt the sting of Russell's tongue. The designer ordered the shutters on the set's houses taken down without consulting the director. They were in an early version of the design, and Russell was expecting them to be in place. The result was "a huge row."

"I can't trust you!" the director shouted. "I can't trust you! In future you're going to bring me everything to be signed."

"He looked like the mad empress from some B movie," Jarman wrote in his journals, "waving his cane, his long hair flowing, wearing a smock and enormous rings on every finger. He left the set shouting to the air . . ."

On another occasion Jarman chose to bite his tongue rather than risk annoying Russell. Looking for a way to illustrate Louis XIII's extravagance, the director asked his designer a simple question. How could he frame the scene to most upset English audiences? Jarman suggested an outdoor dinner sequence with the king blithely shooting peacocks on the lawn between courses.

Russell couldn't think of a way to stage the scene with any degree of realism, short of blowing away real peacocks. "Make some dummies, stand them on the lawn and detonate them," suggested Jarman. No way, countered Russell. Not real enough.

In the end Russell conjured up a memorable scene that began with Jarman's idea but took it to a whole other level. Instead of peacocks, live or otherwise, Russell dressed Huguenot extras as giant blackbirds — imagine a large sports mascots in pointed crow costumes and you get the idea — sprung from oversize cages, running for their lives, pathetically flapping their wings until the king casually guns them down. As one dead Huguenot prisoner collapses into a pond, the amused king mouths the words, "Bye-bye, blackbird."

Dressed in the giant blackbird costume was Harry "Aitch" Fielder, stand-in for Dudley Sutton and "supporting artist." "Another of Ken's little jobs was to dress me up as a giant crow and to get drowned in the Pinewood pond," he wrote on his website. "Now in theory it's quite easy to do. You float in the pond then sink into three foot of water whilst holding a plastic bottle of air in one hand and another one of blood in the other hand . . . simple. As you sink you squeeze the bottles and the air and blood rise to the surface. Now here's the rub. The giant crow's feathers won't let me sink. After about ten minutes the brains on the film come up with Plan B. They will drop a huge weight with a steel ring in it to the bottom of the pond, then tie a rope around my waist under the feathers then through the steel ring."

The other end of the rope was then given to three burly prop men on the other side of the pond who would give the rope a good yank at the proper time, pulling Fielder under. "By now I've been in the water for nearly an hour and I'm getting cold," he continues. "The fish in the pond have got the hump with me and have started nibbling at the feathers and certain other parts of my anatomy. A couple of large brandies help with the cold and we're ready for a take.

"I'm floating on the top and on a cue the prop men will pull me down to the bottom. As I'm releasing air and blood . . . (Big thought) What about my own air supply?! How will the prop men know when I've run out of air to breathe so that they can release the rope? Another large brandy and it's decided that when I pull on the rope they will release it their end. Well to cut an even longer story short, the idea worked and after about six takes (and six more brandies) Ken got what he wanted.

"The moral of this story is, don't mix brandy and water."

"It's marvelous," said Russell of the finished take. "What do you think of that?"

Jarman hated the scene, but chose to stay mum. "I suppose it's OK," he said without enthusiasm. In *Dancing Ledge* he wrote, "The idea had transformed from the steely, vicious concentration of a scene from *The White Devil* into a farce. My sensibilities about what was appropriate were violated."

Jarman wasn't the only one who hated the sequence. The pot shot scene drew a lot of critical fire. The *New York*

Times said, "It's not the fantasy that is objectionable, but the quality of the imagination behind it."

Even one of his cast hated the setup. "He likes very bad jokes," said Sutton of Russell. "I always think the worst joke in that film is 'Bye-bye, blackbird.' It's just a really bad line."

In *An Appalling Talent* Russell defended the scene. "People say to me, 'The king in *The Devils* is ridiculous,' but the things we know about Louis; he was an extravagant homosexual, a great shot, hater of Protestants, lover of shooting blackbirds and dressing as a woman and choreographing his own numbers; all are in the film. I'd used 'bye-bye, blackbird' in [*Isadora*] and it just seemed to tie up naturally with His Majesty's blackbird obsession so I had him say it when he let one have it in the back. I wanted to make everyone realize I wasn't trying to be 'true' in the sense they thought I should be true to what I was showing. I was cocking a snook at people who had preconceived ideas of what a historical film should be."

Russell isn't simply suggesting the king killed Protestants for sport in a most dehumanizing, ridiculous way; he's displaying how detached from reality Louis was. It is a campy and, in almost anyone else's hands, unforgivable scene, but Russell uses it as an allegory of Louis's decadence and an extension of the king's characterization from the startling opening scene.

Painted with the director's trademark libidinous brushstrokes, the opening scene's recreation of the Birth of Venus, with Louis in drag performing the title role, is a mix of Gothic and eroticized images that starts the movie's gears turning on a few levels. More than simply providing an eye-popping, somewhat historically accurate opening, it first and foremost establishes the theatrical feel that permeates the film. Russell transforms Louis's own decadance into a symbol of the corruption of the court of a king who was more interested in fun and games than ruling, a take on the king that only had a passing connection with reality.

To create the soundscape so crucial to the film's unsettling feel, Ken Russell hired a composer who had never before scored a movie. Peter Maxwell Davies (now Sir Peter, Master of the Queen's Music) was the *enfant terrible* of the classical music world, an intense young composer known for shocking audiences and critics. He and Russell were a match made in heaven.

"Ken Russell heard *Eight Songs for a Mad King* [a 1969 modern interpretation of Handel's *Messiah*] and he became interested in my work," Maxwell Davies told me in 2011. "He contacted me and he asked me would I like to write some music for a film? I had never done anything of the kind before. I said, 'What is it?' He said, 'Well, I'm going to do a film based on Aldous Huxley's book.' I knew the book and said, 'Well, that's just my kind of subject.' We met up, as far as I can remember, and we got on fine, and there we were. I was going to do my very first film."

Editor Michael Bradsell told Mark Kermode that Maxwell Davies "was at the avant-garde of classical composers at that time. They weren't going to get a hit single for the soundtrack out of that."

For his part Maxwell Davies says he took the challenge because he was interested in the late medieval and Renaissance periods and, he admitted, "this might sound silly but I was born in 1934 and I thought this is three hundred years exactly before my birth! That kind of thing sometimes does influence you. I thought, 'Let's have a go at this.'"

He and David Munrow, a medieval and Renaissance music specialist, mixed and mingled the music of the period with contemporary classical styles. Munrow supplied the music for the film's masques — Praetorius for King Louis's performance and Gervaise for the peasants' dance at Grandier's execution. Maxwell Davies wrote four sections: "Fantasia on the Dies Irae" (Sister Jeanne's fantasy of Grandier as Christ), the score for Sister Jeanne's meeting with Father Mignon, the Rape of Christ, and the burning at the stake.

"I remember on the set watching great goings-on and Ken Russell would shout out, 'Here we need trombones!' Well, of course I knew damn well we couldn't afford a chorus of trombones so I'd have to do some kind of substitute for it."

He calls working on the film "an extraordinary learning curve." He worked closely with Russell, who provided detailed notes for reference. "I think one of the most remarkable things was that when everything was being edited, he gave me exact lengths of scenes and where the music should change and what it should underline; a script which went down minutes and seconds in very, very great detail.

"On two or three occasions I said, 'Ken, I would like to have a little bit more time here so can you find some more footage so I can finish the musical argument I have started.' And I would find that I would be given perhaps a half minute or a minute more of a shot and that, I think, was very, very helpful."

The creative process leading up to the recording sessions was a bit more solitary, however. "It was one of the very first things I did after coming here to Orkney," he says of his home in remote northern Scotland. "I wrote that in winter in a house on a cliff there with no electricity. A very, very violent winter. It was quite something to do. It was all written under, I suppose you could call them, quite extraordinary circumstances. There aren't many composers who would go to a place like that to just concentrate absolutely on writing that music in the winter. I gathered wood on the beach for fire and I kept it going and I had candles and oil lamps. But it was an extreme thing to do, I think, to write that music."

Using Russell's notes, he wrote the score "in a house with no piano, just in the dark with my head. You hear everything, plainly, clearly; you don't need a piano.

"It's as if when you hear it in your head it's a little bit faint, but everything is there, but when you actually hear it in the flesh, it all springs to life. It's a lovely experience. It still is. I suppose it's like when you write a letter you don't say the words to yourself, but you can hear them and you know exactly what you've written. It's the same with music except that it is a great deal more elaborate and on many lines and many instruments. But you still know what it is and what it sounds like."

As he wrote he tried, as much as possible, to get inside the heads of the characters in the film. "You are that part when you are writing it. You take over the personality. I think the music is inside the heads of those people."

He was also inspired by Jarman's sets. "I realized with that marvelous set Derek created that this has got to sound as if it is taking place in a public toilet," he told Kermode. "A sound that comes louder than it is because it comes echoing back at you and it begins to have a resonance you want to get out of. There's a slight feeling that you don't want to stay there too long."

Back in London the music was performed by David Munrow's group of Renaissance players and Fires of London, Maxwell Davies' group with, he says, "some extras thrown in so we could have trombone and occasionally some other instruments. Of course we made it sound different by treating the sound to make it sound fuller."

"It was all very exciting," he said, but as it did for so many others on the production, the heaviness of the material began to wear on him. "Yes, it was a very, very dark place," he said. "I think you had to distance yourself from it, because it could take over and become so dark that you wouldn't want to work on it. In order that that shouldn't happen, and you have to be rather careful, you have to be rather technical and think about the technical aspects of it, because all the feeling, all the emotion, all the identification happens when you are actually writing it and that is, indeed, very dark.

"When you're actually in the studio recording the music all you think about is, does it fit? Do you have to change things? Is this adequate? Get the timing right. Does that happen precisely where it should? All those technical things do help you get through the very practical thing of laying the score down in the recording."

Occasionally Maxwell Davies resorted to some very unconventional techniques. During the recording of the music for the burning at the stake scene, he instructed one of the percussion players to scrape his fingers against a blackboard. Mixed in with the score it is barely perceptible, but "I think the effect is there," he said.

"I do remember that we recorded that music with the film showing in the studio in black and white. After we'd played it, and I was conducting it and it all fit perfectly, we came to view it and the players were actually very, very moved by the music. Just the music playing with that grainy, black-and-white film. It was quite an experience."

Some of the musicians were even in tears at the end of that recording session. "I was surprised and very pleased. I thought, 'Well, something's coming across in the images and the music and it is blending and making something.'"

Maxwell Davies worked on two films with Russell (he followed *The Devils* with *The Boy Friend*) and recalled his initial feeling upon meeting the director: "It was clear he had great respect for music as such and so I thought, 'He sounds so promising to work with.' And indeed so, as it turned out."

Chapter Five

DIRECTING *THE DEVILS*

"His majesty triumphs again!"
— off-camera voice

Russell's method of working with actors wasn't always traditional. He didn't like line readings — instructing an actor on how to say a line by speaking it for them — or discussing motivation. As his friend and confidant Leonard Pollack explained, "He hires professionals and expects them to do it."

Murray Melvin, who worked with Russell five times, suggested it would be impossible to sum up the director's style. "That's writing a book," he told me. "I could not describe that to you in a couple of lines. That's a long journey, but I mean painting pictures is a lot. To go any more than that would be silly because it would make it sound trite but it isn't trite. It's very deep."

Dudley Sutton added a bit of color to the discussion of Russell's methods. "All that motivation stuff and Stanislavski is rubbish," he said. "Ken would have said, 'Never mind the acting; get on with the fucking film!'"

A *Time* magazine piece described his on-set behavior. "'He's doing a von Stroheim again' go the whispers when he explodes over a misplaced prop or demands that costumes be sewn overnight. One long-suffering colleague, when asked what kind of childhood Russell had, rolled his eyes to the ceiling and replied, 'He's having it now.'"

No, he'll never be described as being an actor's director, but he did have his methods of dealing with actors.

Gemma Jones remembered Russell bringing out the best

in her performance, although it didn't feel that way at the time. "We filmed up in the Lake District, very, very beautiful," she said. "Filming near Bamborough Castle it was terribly cold. I remember being really ill. I had the flu, I think, shivering in my caravan and then having to stand out on an island and [Russell] was frightfully unsympathetic. Then when I looked at it I looked rather lovely, sort of pale and wan. You'd have no idea I was feeling like death warmed up."

On the set of *Mahler* he used some life-threatening trickery to pull a performance out of one of the younger actors. Just before cameras were set to roll on a complicated scene in a lake, Gary Rich, the actor playing the young Mahler, told Russell he didn't know how to swim.

"That's perfectly all right, young man," Russell reassured him, leaving out that the scene was actually a near-drowning scene, which, the director deadpanned, Rich "executed to perfection."

"He was a bit of a bugger, Ken was," Judith Paris told me. "There was one sequence where we were on our knees in the main chapel area and he wouldn't let us wear knee pads and we knelt all day on a concrete floor. I thought, 'Why, Ken? We can act pain.'"

As nontraditional as his methods were, they got results. On the set of *Crimes of Passion*, for example, he manipulated Kathleen Turner, fresh off the mainstream Hollywood success of *Romancing the Stone*, into doing a scene the way he wanted her to do it.

"There was a scene where she gives a guy head," said Pollack, "the scene where she wipes her mouth and delivers a line. Ken was having a hard time with her. She had a big, big head and now she's giving head. Ken realized that she was reluctant to do certain things even though she signed to do the film and it was all in the script. So for that scene he told her, 'Okay, Kathleen, you've just finished giving him head. We cut to you and you do a big swallow, wipe your mouth and do your line.'"

"I don't want to do that," she said. "I'm not going to do a big gulp swallow, that'll be disgusting. Half the audience would leave."

"Let's get another opinion," Russell said, calling in the film's writer/producer Barry Sandler. The director explained the problem to Sandler who thought about it and said, "Ken, I'm sorry to say, but I have to agree with Kathleen."

Russell said, "Okay, here's what we'll do. You pull away. You wipe your mouth and say your line."

Turner agreed and walked away.

Russell then said to Sandler, "Thanks, that's all I wanted her to do in the first place, but if I had started with that she'd have fought me on that."

"He doesn't give in to them," said Pollack. "In other words he's not an ass licker with his actors. I've heard him call Georgina Hale a 'fucking cunt' on set. 'You fucking cunt, you'll dance in those boots! Women have danced in them for years! Don't tell me you can't dance in them.' That was in *Mahler* when she was dancing with his coffin."

By the time Russell was shooting *The Devils*, he was a big-time director, comfortable rolling lots of film. Not a Kubrickian number of takes per scene — it's rumored Stanley Kubrick once made Scatman Crothers shoot a simple over-the-shoulder shot 148 times — but more than the average 6:1 or 10:1 shot ratio (the total duration of the footage shot versus the length of the final cut) used on most features. "Ken, certainly round about that time, often did many takes," said Bradsell, "but it was a combination of maybe the artists slipping up somewhere, or if it was a complicated camera move it may have to be cut because the follow focus cameraman [the first assistant cameraman] reckoned he hadn't followed properly or whatever. It was always justified; it wasn't a question of, we've got fifty takes here, they all look alike, which one should we choose."

Judith Paris remembered that Russell "knew what he wanted but he had a deeply depressing habit of doing take sixteen, take seventeen, eighteen . . . you'd do take twenty-three and he'd say, 'Do it again like you did on take five.' You'd say, 'It's gone. Completely gone. I've no idea. We've been doing it so many different ways I can't remember.'"

Despite the large number of takes, and her frustration with having to repeat her performances, Paris said she trusted her director. "You'd look around and think, 'My God, that framing is wonderful. It doesn't matter what I do, the picture is so perfect and he'll create a performance for me in the editing suite.' He was very much convinced of that philosophy, that performances can be made."

Vincent Winter, a former child star who worked as an unaccredited assistant director on the film, offered an explanation for Russell burning through so much film. "Ken is a very deep man, a very intuitive man. Although he's prepared, he will develop a scene if he thinks there is a better direction in it. He is, I think, an excessive man also."

As the shoot dragged on, Reed continued to be a handful as usual. The very thing that made Reed perfect for the role — his individuality — also made him a squeaky wheel on set.

Though Reed was notorious for being a difficult actor, the rapport between Reed and Russell allowed them to work together often, while other directors were leery of using him. His reputation often preceded him. Yet at least one director discovered that Reed's reputation for being difficult was a tad overhyped.

David Cronenberg directed Oliver Reed in the 1979 cult classic *The Brood*. In 2011 he spoke to me about what it was like working with the troublesome actor. "I had heard all kinds of things about how incredibly difficult and destructive he was on set. Things like don't ever go out for dinner with him because he'll get drunk and do terrible, embarrassing things . . . scary, embarrassing things. There was one time someone told me about him out for dinner with Susan George. He took her food and put it on the floor, under the table and told her to get on her hands and knees and eat it there like a dog.

"All of these things were pretty convincing so on that level I was worried. I was just a young, relatively inexperienced director with a very limited budget and a very limited schedule so I really didn't have time for any sort of actor misbehaving. The thing you worry about most is how much time that might eat up on your set."

Reed lived down to his reputation when, the moment he got into Toronto, he was promptly stopped by police when he walked across Avenue Road in nothing but his underwear. Cronenberg got a call that Reed had been arrested, but later discovered the report was erroneous (the police laughed and helped him back to his hotel room when they realized who he was). The next day was the costume fitting, where the director usually meets the stars for the first time, and Cronenberg dreaded meeting the rowdy actor. "But to my total shock and pleasant surprise," he says, "it was like meeting what I would have assumed from Laurence Olivier. He was incredible polite, proper, completely clear and professional. Very sweet. We just discussed the costumes like you would in a professional manner and he was trying them on and he was completely fine. I thought, 'I don't know what's going on, but I'm happy to have this.' And that's how he was on the shoot."

During the shoot, Cronenberg thought Reed was very professional. Cronenberg reports that Reed would offer up suggestions like, "'Watch that my eyes don't go crossed . . . Sometimes if you do a close-up one of my eyes will wander and then my eyes will be crossed.' . . . That's completely normal and of course he had magnificent eyes and a magnificent voice.

"There was only one night we were shooting very late and we had children playing these little creatures and he said, 'I think we should stop shooting. I think everybody is exhausted. I think it's not good for the children.' He said, 'Make me the villain. Stop shooting and say I refused to shoot. I'm not refusing to shoot, but I'm telling you I don't think this is good. You can blame me.' We did stop shooting and he was completely right. It often happens. You keep going and everybody's exhausted and not working well, and yes, we had children. So even that was not anything bad.

"There was one other time when we switched some schedule so that we were shooting a scene he wasn't prepared for. He said, 'This is going to be difficult for me. I just want to tell you that because you know my reputation.' I thought, 'Uh-oh.' He said, 'Yes, my reputation. I'm letter-perfect.'

"Of course I didn't say, 'That isn't really your reputation. Your reputation is that you're a monster.' He said, 'You see I have a technique of working that I've developed which is that just before I go to bed I read it and I take it to heart and I sleep on it. In the morning I have the dialogue perfectly. I haven't been able to do this today because you switched the schedules so I'm going to need some help.'

"And he was absolutely right. It was a lot of dialogue and I had to do a lot of takes to get him through it because he was blowing his lines, although he would get them all wonderfully sooner or later . . . this is not unusual. But he was absolutely right because this was the only time on the shoot that he ever was in this kind of trouble. It was wonderful because some actors get embarrassed and won't ask you for help and they'll start to be hostile and angry but they are really just angry at themselves. He didn't do that. He just said, 'I'm going to need your help to get through this.' Having said that, it was easy. All it meant was, well, I'm going to be cutting back and forth between these two people anyway so we'll just keep doing it until we get it. He was fine with that. He didn't punish me for it, let's put it that way. Which I've had other actors do.

"I remember [the late Canadian film historian and interviewer] Brian Linehan telling me some story about going to visit Oliver Reed in a hotel and he said Reed just had young women lined up one after the other and was having sex with them one after the other. Which, we all say, great! No problem there. Fine for them and fine for him but Brian's sense of it was that he was basically pretty bored with it all. Although he was doing it and it was pretty perfunctory . . . this was Brian's take on it. But he never brought any of that to the set. Ever. Of course I wasn't going to call him on the weekends so that was never a problem.

"I always thought he was a fantastic actor. That voice, wow, what a voice. Also his face, just a presence, so powerful."

To Cronenberg, Reed was a perfect gentleman. But a decade earlier, playing a role for a director he knew so well, Reed could still be trouble for Ken Russell. To prep for the torture scene in *The Devils* Reed was told to shave all the hair from his head and legs, a request he accepted, according to Cliff Goodwin's book *Evil Spirits*, "without a murmur." His voice raised above a murmur, however, when Russell added that Reed's eyebrows would have to go as well. Reed refused in no uncertain terms.

"We might as well not do the movie at all," Russell roared in response, his arms flailing in the wind.

"Don't be bloody silly," Reed said. "It can't make all that much difference."

"Of course it's important," Russell replied. "They shaved off all of Grandier's bodily hair and then stuck hot pokers up his arse."

The perverseness of the image appealed to Reed's darker side and he agreed to the shave job but with a proviso. "All right," he said, "but I want them insured for half a million pounds in case they don't grow back properly." Lloyd's of London, who had previously insured silent film comedian Ben Turpin's eyes against uncrossing, Jimmy Durante's nose and, in their most famous case, the *Titanic*, was contacted and took the claim. The eyebrows later "grew back abundantly," Russell told the *Observer*, "for which the insurers were very grateful."

Production carried on until the next day, when a freshly shaved Reed announced to producer Roy Baird that he was quitting the movie. The producer, who had worked with Reed before as associate producer on *Women in Love*, and was familiar with Reed's tomfoolery, asked what the problem was.

Reed explained that the script was in a constant state of flux as Russell made almost daily changes. The latest outrage was the inclusion of long speeches in Latin. Russell, in an attempt to create a realistic portrayal of the ceremonies that would have been performed in Loudun in the period, hired an academic to translate parts of the script into seventeenth-century Latin. The changes infuriated Reed who found the additions hard to read and awkward to pronounce.

According to Goodwin's *Evil Spirits*, he ranted, "I'm not a scholar. If I wanted to be a scholar, I would have gone to Cambridge. The only reason I didn't go to university was because I can't spell, I can't add up and I can't sodding well stand Latin. Now I want off this film because I didn't sign up to read a script that was full of Latin. So tell Ken Russell to piss off."

A Reed temper tantrum was a thing not to be taken lightly, so the next day Russell — wearing his now trademark Donald Duck cap over his long gray hair — sheepishly told the actor that he had been thinking about the Latin and had come to the conclusion that except for a few short lines they could cut it from the script. Reed thanked the director, adding, "I was getting a bit worried about it."

Instead of learning the Latin lines by heart, Reed relied on an old actor's trick. In a scene where he was required to chant in Latin while anointing his congregation with holy water, he wrote his lines on scraps of paper, which he floated in the water and kept out of camera range.

That scene went flawlessly, but he wasn't so lucky in another, more complicated scene. Russell blocked the absolution-of-the-dead prayer scene — a shot showing Father Grandier kneeling, breaking bread and beginning the prayer, "*Non intres in judicium cum servo tuo Domine*" — to be filmed completely in profile. Reed was to close his eyes, bow his head and intone the words.

They did the first take, and Russell was dumbfounded. Reed had said the difficult dialogue perfectly. "And you told me you couldn't learn all that Latin," Russell said proudly. In take two Russell caught on to Reed's trick when he noticed something off about the shot. Through the viewfinder he saw Reed's face was slightly contorted. A closer look revealed that the actor had tightly shut the eye closest to the camera while the far eye was twitching, straining to stay open a crack to read the lines, which Reed had written on the bread. "That won't do," Russell chastised and sent Reed back to his trailer to properly learn his lines.

Despite their differences, Reed said, "I remember noticing the gleam in [Russell's] eye while everybody was working away on the set, so I knew something good was going on."

And with Russell's direction, Reed managed to make Grandier sympathetic: a sinning spiritual leader transformed into someone doomed to die for his beliefs. *The Devils* is a career high for him. He stands tall in a movie whose pitch and performances are dialed up to eleven.

Russell pushed the actors toward the outlandish, but in this case the uninhibited performances fit the tone of the movie. It's a piece that demands strong, heavy-handed performances and Reed delivered.

During filming, Reed was giving the performance of a lifetime but was also pushing the boundaries, personally and professionally. Wherever Reed went chaos followed, but it was his insistence on authenticity in one scene that put the entire film in jeopardy.

Unlike his rival Richard Harris — who once didn't bathe for weeks to play the role of a filthy person — Reed was not a method actor. In fact, as this story from *Gladiator* actor Omid Djalili shows, he often took the chance to take the mickey out of anyone making the method actor claim. "There's a bit where the director said he's got to grab your balls," Djalili said on the BBC program *Top Gear* in June 2005. "And [Reed] said, 'Are you a method actor?' And I said, 'Well, yes.' And he said, 'You don't mind if I really grab your balls?' and he put his hand out and held my balls [gestures with outstretched left hand]. And when they said, 'Action!' he held it. Then, when they said 'Cut!' he's still holding onto my balls. And he did his five takes having a cup of tea [gestures sipping tea with right hand while left hand still outstretched] and I just stood there saying, 'Yes, Mr. Oliver Reed.'"

Reed was no fan of method acting or method actors, but when it came to Grandier's death scene, the burning at the stake, he took a method technique to dangerous lengths.

It is a nightmarish sequence, more viscerally disturbing than the Rape of Christ scene, which cuts away from the nun's shenanigans to provide some relief from the madness. The burning scene, on the other hand, is a full metal jacket onslaught. Russell packs each frame with mocking faces, skull masks, Grandier's quickly melting skin and flames, flames, flames.

As the flames rise, Grandier hears a fired-up crowd cheering his demise. Philippe Trincant's father yells, "Burn! Burn!" while her new husband holds Grandier's newborn baby aloft to get a better look at the flaming man. "See how your mother's honor was avenged!" Adds Grandpa Trincant, "Lucky little bastard. It's not every day baby sees daddy burned to death!"

Grandier's death is detailed by Russell's camera, shooting through the flames to show his bubbling, melting skin, then reversing the shot to Grandier's point of view, noting the cheering crowd and the pantomime dancers reenacting his indiscretions. Peter Maxwell Davies' music accompanies the painful squawks to fill the soundtrack. As Grandier roasts faster than a Christmas turkey in a microwave, de Laubardemont walks into the frame, nods, and the walls come down, scattering the crowd. Grandier is gone and with him goes the safety and sanctity of Loudun.

Despite the fact that Christopher Hobbs had fabricated a half-burnt Oliver Reed latex dummy for use in the scene, the actor insisted on making the shot look as realistic as possible. To this end he came up with the idea of rigging a trapdoor inside the funeral pyre. The idea was to light the whole thing ablaze as Russell called action. Reed would react to the situation, watching in fear as the flames edged their way toward him. It would make for a convincing and terrifying shot.

"That was a very complicated special effects [shot] but

it was done brilliantly by a man called John Richardson," said Vincent Winter. "The pyre was built in such a way to have gas jets throughout the whole of the space and the gas would turn the flame up between the camera and the actor. Sometimes we would have to get in very close to Oliver and simply put a gas jet in front of his face with the camera shooting at him. He was very brave and stood it as long as he could and then said no more."

As they shot the scene Reed waited for the fire to reach waist height. As a "very strange smell" came from his legs he hit the release button for the trapdoor. Unfortunately the catch didn't release — the wooden trapdoor had swollen shut in the heat — and Reed was left at the mercy of the flames until the studio firemen doused the fire.

"The only time I can remember him being in actual dis-comfort was when we burned him at the stake," Russell said in 1996. "He did get a bit hot." Perhaps it was this incident Reed was referring to when he said the four months spent making *The Devils* took four years off his life. "It was certainly the most difficult and the most strenuous part I have ever played," he said.

There's a great deal of controversy surrounding Vanessa Redgrave's work in the film as well. Some people "didn't much go for Vanessa," said Judith Paris. "She was very detached from the part."

Sister Jeanne is one of the trickiest roles in the piece. It would be easy to overreach in the part, simply playing the nun as a lunatic with a jones for a man she's never met in the flesh, but Redgrave creates a character out of the mad-ness. Her movie-star good looks contrast with the hump on her back and the bug in her brain to help create a complete portrait of a person who is filled with pain and anger and who enjoys the attention she gets from her wild accusations. For possibly the first time in her life someone is interested in her. It's the wrong kind of interest and from the wrong people — Barre and de Laubardemont — and the consequences are high, but Redgrave humanizes Jeanne, making us believe that this repulsive woman is just a human being. It's an unhinged performance, her head bent cruelly to one side as a result of severe spinal curvature in her upper back, the exact opposite of the typical upright religious figure seen in films of the era. In one scene she scolds the nuns, like an early incarnation of Dana Carvey's Church Lady, before emitting a demented laugh that suggests all is not right in Reverend-Mother land.

In the *Observer* Russell said, "Vanessa Redgrave was up for anything in the script. She was one of the least bothersome actresses I could ever wish for: she just threw herself into it and really enjoyed the experience. I think she found it somewhat liberating to let herself go, which she certainly did." Just before his death in 2011 Russell heaped more praise on Redgrave, writing in the *Times* that watching the performance is akin to seeing "an oil painting by Brueghel or Bosch come to life before your eyes."

Kudos too go to Dudley Sutton for creating one of the great screen villains. His mincing but Machiavellian take on Baron de Laubardemont is filled with menace. He is a man unconcerned with consequences because he has, so he thinks, God and the king on his side. He acts with impunity, strutting through his scenes with a calculated sense of entitlement. Sutton personifies the evil at work in the film; he's mad, bad and, for Grandier, dangerous to know.

Only Gemma Jones stands apart from the crowd, delivering a simple performance befitting her character, ripe with beauty and decency, which must cut through the madness surrounding her.

While the primary actors found it difficult to work on the set, it was no walk in the park for the much-maligned extras either. In his journal Jarman recalled a "revolting afternoon at the plague pit."

It's been suggested that the plague scenes had a direct influence on *Monty Python and the Holy Grail*, but an email exchange with Terry Gilliam put that rumor to rest. "I don't think *The Devils* had any influence on us," he wrote. "Pity."

Heavily made-up background actors — they were painted off-white and gray, covered in Rice Krispies and finished off with dabs of red and yellow — were layered, literally on top of one another, marinating in gallons of fake blood. Trouble was, the blood attracted "clouds of wasps," which made the extras jittery and unable to lie still and play dead. In an effort to save the shot Russell ordered a change and got rid of the fake blood. "In the end he made me bring bottles of ketchup from the kitchen," Jarman wrote, "which made everything worse as the wasps preferred it to the real thing."

The plague extras also had another unforeseen hardship: they had to stay on set to eat. Because of the heavy makeup — sores and peeling skin — they weren't welcomed with open arms at the crew restaurant. Apparently the sight of them put others off their food. One extra dared to venture into the diner fully made up. "The canteen was packed when I entered but within seconds I had a table to myself," said Aitch Fielder. "I wonder why?"

The extras, for the most part, stayed on set. The same couldn't be said of Shirley Russell, the director's wife, muse and costume designer on nine of his features (*Women in Love, The Music Lovers, The Devils, The Boy Friend, Savage Messiah, Mahler, Tommy, Lisztomania* and *Valentino*). She worked on thirty-seven films throughout her career, her last being *Shackleton* for Charles Sturridge in 2001.

In her obituary (she passed away of cancer in 2002) the

Times trumpeted her ability to "date any portrait from its clothing to within a year or two, and [she] was frequently consulted by museums and art dealers on questions of attribution. She pioneered the use of real, historic clothes in her films, and would tour the country searching auctioned wardrobes, jumble sales and thrift shops to build up an incomparable collection of twentieth-century costume."

"Look at darling Shirley Russell's costumes," said Melvin. "Wow. Wow. They are just so staggering aren't they? My soutane that she did for me . . . My goodness me, I used to step into that and I didn't have to do anything. Put on Shirley's costumes and you're the part. With that haircut and the costume I used to look in the mirror in my dressing room and think, 'Oh, yeah, all right. What are the words Murray, because everything else is there.'"

After her time working with Russell, she received Oscar nominations for her costuming in *Agatha* and *Reds*, but on the set of *The Devils* she was desperately unhappy. She brought her usual attention to detail to the project, however, carefully blending period details with Russell's ideas of injecting a hint of modernity into the look of the film.

Costume designer Leonard Pollack worked with the Russells on *Mahler*, *Tommy* and *Valentino* and became a member of their inside circle. "Her work? It's brilliant. The only thing I wasn't crazy about was the tape she used on the hoods. The crosses on the hoods. I guess it was done at the last minute and I guess they had to use tape but the whole thing is theatrical. It doesn't matter."

Soon, however, the chaotic shoot became too much and during one particularly intense day she stormed off. Russell, as usual, was blasting loud aggressive music on set to create a mood for the actors when she left. Dramatically leaving the set wasn't unusual for her. "I do tend to walk out," she told Gordon Gow of *Films and Filming*. "When we're filming there's a different sort of relationship between Ken and myself. There's a 'them' and 'us' feeling: 'them' being the production unit and 'us' being the wardrobe department. It's very strange. It's hysterical really. I often disappear for days and won't go near the place and they have to try and coax me back."

"She was a target for Ken," Leonard Pollack told me in 2011. He didn't work on *The Devils*, but supplies insight to the director's treatment of his wife. "Shirley and I were both targets for Ken. When he needed to lose his temper and couldn't take it out on whoever he really needed to take it out on, he would take it out on Shirley and me, because he knew we would not take it personally. Except maybe Shirley did. I know she was always upset after he did and so was I. I mean he would scream at me for something I didn't even know what he was talking about.

"He's not like an actor's director, you realize. He doesn't sit down with them and tell them what to do, where their motivation is coming from. He expects them to know that. But if he is not getting what he has in his head, and he's not very good at communicating those things to other people, he would call Shirley or me, if I was around, if she was around, onto the set and lash out at us without us even knowing what the fuck he was talking about. He'd humiliate me or Shirley in front of everybody. Then immediately go into a take. So the actors had no fucking idea what they were doing, he got something totally fresh and new, something they weren't practicing in mirrors and stuff and it was usually what he wanted. He wanted something spontaneous and real and it threw everybody off."

The director soon began to suspect something more was at play than simply set politics. After Shirley's sudden departure he started to connect the dots between her frequent "driving lessons" and her absence. "These lessons often extended well into the afternoon," he wrote in his autobiography, "as I discovered whenever I sent word for her to join us on the set to discuss one of her bizarre costumes and explain, for instance, which way round it should be worn. Shirley was never to be found and, although there was nothing unusual in that because as the director's wife she was a law unto herself, it nevertheless started me wondering if a little back seat driving might be involved."

In the end he couldn't blame her for running off (temporarily) with the chauffeur given the brutal atmosphere on set. "Small wonder Shirley was driven off the sound stage to seek peace with one not caught up in the torture, violence and death. Nor is it surprising that both our faith and our marriage began to crumble. It was altogether a disturbing experience, and so, indeed, was the film itself."

By leaps and bounds the most controversial scene in *The Devils* is the wild nunsploitation orgy, commonly referred to as the Rape of Christ. It is the legendary scene thought lost for more than three decades; a few hundred feet of film caused Ken Russell more aggravation than all his other movies put together. Explicit, inflammatory and groundbreaking, it mixed sexual activity and religion — a longstanding cinema taboo — and can only be described as orgiastic. The riotous orgy/exorcism scene is a vital sequence in the film as it illustrates Russell's themes of political, religious and sexual corruption.

The original plan was for the scene to follow Father Barre's exorcism of the Ursuline nuns using a holy relic provided by the king. Barre waves what he believes to be a vial of Christ's blood over the nuns and they soon calm down; the demons appear to leave their bodies. When the relic is proven to be a hoax, the most notorious scene of the 1970s really kicks into gear. While Father Mignon watches and masturbates from afar, the frantic nuns strip Barre before using a life-sized crucifix, complete with an effigy of Jesus, as a giant sex toy. In Russell's words, "[They] throw themselves on it, having it in every possible way."

The giant crucifix was one of the few pieces in the film not designed by Derek Jarman. The creation of the scene's central prop was left to sculptor Christopher Hobbs, a mutual friend of Russell and Jarman. "Derek's background was very similar to mine and somehow we were exactly the same age so we got on quite well and went on from there really," Hobbs told documentary filmmaker Andy Kimpton-Nye. "I'd actually worked with Ken Russell for a long time before [*The Devils*]. I'd been making props for Ken Russell way back into the television period."

Using as inspiration artist Matthias Grünewald's *Isenheim Altarpiece* — a sixteenth-century artifact now on display at the Unterlinden Museum at Colmar, Alsace — Hobbs designed a massive crucifix constructed out of polystyrene with a gesso finish.

Russell's visualization of the scene from Aldous Huxley's book was meant to come at the end of a series of possession scenes, a climax to represent "the rape of the church, the rape of Christ." But no matter what the intention, setting images to the debauched scene described in Huxley's tome would be a challenge for Russell, who noted that unlike the author's words the images would be "immediate, irrefutable." And, as it turns out, controversial.

"You have to understand it is a ballet," Melvin told me. "Ken trained as a classical dancer and the whole thing [the Rape of Christ scene] is a ballet that came out of Ken's dance imagination. When we were doing it he played the *Rite of Spring* [dramatic pause] very, very loudly on that huge stage. He had lots of dancers in his company and although all those bits were done separately, he joined them all together in this huge, wonderful ballet. It is one, in my opinion, may I say, one of the great sequences on film."

While casting for the controversial scenes, Russell and company were very careful to let everyone know what would be expected of them once filming commenced. "When we were sent the script I think all the nuns were told to read, specifically, certain scenes," said Imogen Claire (an uncredited nun) in *Hell on Earth*, "and if they weren't prepared to do what the scenes described, they shouldn't accept the job. The scenes described quite graphically what was going to be required."

Judith Paris, who played Sister Agnes, remembered it differently. "None of the nuns knew there was going to be nudity. It wasn't in the original script."

The actors and extras participating in the possession sequences and the soon-to-be-infamous Rape of Christ shoot were also given photocopies of contemporary accounts of the possessions at Loudun as background material to help them understand Russell's twisted vision. The excerpts described the nuns' behavior: the tearing of clothes, the nudity, the contortion of their bodies into overtly sexual positions and other extreme conduct.

"It was authentic descriptions of the nuns' behavior under interrogation," Paris told me in 2011. "So it was fairly graphic. For a while after Grandier had been arrested the nuns were put on display at these great open-air events and people would come from the countryside to witness the devils being driven out of the nuns in a very public and explicit way. It's all there in the *Dictionary of Witchcraft*."

An example of the type of description is found in Des Niau's 1634 book *The History of The Devils of Loudun: The Alleged Possession of the Ursuline Nuns, and the Trial and Execution of Urbain Grandier, Told by an Eye-Witness.*

> [The nuns] struck their chests and backs with their heads, as if they had their necks broken, and with inconceivable rapidity; they twisted their arms at the joints of the shoulder, the elbow or the wrist, two or three times around. Lying on their stomachs, they joined the palms of their hands to the soles of their feet; their faces became so frightful one could not bear to look at them; their eyes remained open without winking. Their tongues issued suddenly from their mouths, horribly swollen, black, hard and covered with pimples, and yet while in this state they spoke distinctly. They threw themselves back till their heads touched their feet, and walked in this position with wonderful rapidity, and for a long time. They uttered cries so horrible and so loud that nothing like it was ever heard before. They made use of expressions so indecent as to shame the most debauched of men, while their acts, both in exposing themselves and inviting lewd behavior from those present, would have astonished the inmates of the lowest brothels in the country.

Before cameras rolled, Russell met with the extras one more time to make explicit what was expected of them. Many would have to appear naked, he explained. There would be flagellation and anyone playing a nun would have to have her head and pubic hair shaved for £150 in extra pay, or "naked nun money" as executive producer Roy Baird called it. As an added bonus, producers offered two wigs to each of the soon-to-be-bald nuns.

"It was before nudity contracts," said Paris, "and this all happened within the first week that we realized what was going to be asked of us, which was not completely apparent in the script. Now, as I've said, some nuns were perfectly happy with that and others weren't. Equity came along to try to sort it out and in the end they came to a financial compromise. Five pounds for tits and ten pounds for the lot including pubic hair and fannies [English slang for female genitals]. Some of them shaved their heads. Some of them found it quite liberating."

Russell wasn't fooling around when he warned the extras about appearing naked. Shooting the sequence and other possession scenes required an almost unprecedented amount of nudity — full frontal and otherwise — from the cast.

"Ken's attitude toward naked women is one of joy and my attitude is the same," said Dudley Sutton in *Hell on Earth*. In a separate interview, he told me how he helped accommodate the naked nuns. "I was the tit warmer," he said. "They danced around a tree I think [most likely this was Sister Jeanne's suicide scene], and as they came running off the set I had two hairdryers and I was warming their breasts. The girls said it was wonderful because that's where they get the most cold."

"I honestly don't remember Dudley's hairdryer," said Imogen Claire in *Hell on Earth*, "but my tits weren't very big. I think he might have gone for the bigger titties."

According to legend, magnums of champagne were served at breakfast to loosen up the cast for the most frenzied of the possession scenes — the Rape of Christ. One cast member remembered it differently.

"He wheeled in the drinks trolley," Judith Paris said in 2011. "It wasn't champagne; it was all kinds of strange things. I never got champagne. It was things like crème de menthe and sherry. At nine o'clock in the morning!"

To further set the mood Russell had four large speakers

hidden on set. For most of the shoot he had been playing the majestic grand finale of Sergei Prokofiev's *The Fiery Angel* — music of "religious dementia" Russell called it — to establish the proper shock and awe atmosphere on set. But when he yelled "action" during the Rape of Christ shoot, the speakers rumbled to life blasting "the most barbaric bit of [Igor Stravinsky's] *The Rite of Spring*," said Jarman, "the music to which I had danced naked myself in my parents' home and played it flat out. Without it, the nuns were simply unable to cope; they were totally inhibited."

Jarman said Russell also had "a drum kit brought in and drum[med] away to whip up fervor."

Background actor Aitch Fielder remembered "a bevy of young girls dressed as nuns walking around the set topless. Reg Prince, who was Oliver Reed's stand-in, said to me, 'Stop looking Aitch, or you'll go blind.' I said, 'I'll risk one eye.'"

That kind of boorish attitude didn't sit well with all the female extras and actors who felt exposed and vulnerable, particularly while the cameras were rolling. "You've got to remember that the film business is very priggish," said Dudley Sutton. "Especially when sex is concerned. If you bare a woman's breast they start closing the county down for miles around, and then all these people start appearing who weren't behind the camera before. Suddenly there are thirty guys all hanging around trying to get a look at some parts of a naked woman. People ripped a hole in the set so they could peer through. It was very odd. It was just a bunch of young girls with no clothes on jumping about trying to pretend being hysterical."

Fielder added that "after the first couple of days it was back to looking at the *Racing Post*," but naked nuns were already on edge.

"I personally was very alarmed for the younger nuns,

because some of them had been told that the film of *The Boy Friend* was coming up shortly and they were obviously desperate to be on that as well," Paris told me. "So there was a lot of 'If I behave myself and do what I'm asked to do on this, maybe I'll get cast.'

"The choreographer was the same, Terry Gilbert. He became Ken's sort of mad familiar. Ken used Terry to do all his dirty work with the nuns. There were scenes of, shall we say politely, excess, and Terry, who was wonderful at getting people going — he was a real party animal as it were — would get things going for Ken. He also had a very loyal wife, Celina, and about three or four other nuns who were extroverts and they led the group's carrying-on. Some of us would hide. Some of us would be doing it."

However, in the passion of the moment, some of the male extras got carried away and were unnecessarily rough and groped the younger, naked female extras.

Bradsell added, "There were some elements among the crowd artists, I don't know whether they were just bored or thought that with all these naked young women around nobody's going to notice if I make an inappropriate gesture or tweak their bottom or whatever. Some of the girls who played nuns and even some of the principals were complaining that they were being interfered with by the crowds."

"There was madness in the air," said Judith Paris. "I wasn't involved with that particular shoot that day. But I came in the next day and I heard the stories of the nuns, naked, running out among the extras and the extras were being coached to fondle them. One girl had an extra putting his . . . anyway, it got out of hand."

Jarman also alleged in his journal that the extras caused other sorts of trouble on set. "They were as stubborn as mules," Jarman wrote. "They insist on wearing watches, never take off their rings, carry newspapers around which come out the moment Ken shouts, 'Cut!' along with knitting and the crosswords."

I asked Bradsell, who spent literally hundreds of hours combing over the rushes, if he noticed any wristwatches on the arms of seventeenth-century nuns. "In terms of anachronisms or any other visual mistakes I don't remember seeing anything like that in rushes at all. But even so, we usually had such vast coverage that if something like that had occurred it would have been a minor annoyance. It wouldn't have ruined the possibility of making a good scene out of it."

One of the extras was a little more high profile than the rest. Leslie Hornby, better known as Twiggy, the "Face of 1966," and her manager-boyfriend Justin de Villeneuve make uncredited appearances. After four years of being the world's most famous model, Twiggy retired, saying, "You can't be a clothes hanger for your entire life!" With aspirations of becoming an actress, she approached The Beatles to back a film of William Faulkner's *The Hanging Tree*. That idea never came to fruition, but Paul McCartney suggested they contact Ken Russell, who encouraged her to pursue and study acting, voice and dance. Her first job was as an extra in *The Devils*.

In *Directing Film*, Russell quotes Twiggy, complete with Cockney vernacular, talking about her cameo. "We woz a couple of King Louis' courtiers in the Rape of Christ scene in the cathedral. I was dressed as a boy and Justin woz in eight-inch 'igh 'eels with cupid bow lips and a blonde wig."

The pair was there at Russell's invitation but high-tailed it off the set when the nuns started stripping. They're clearly visible (look to the left of Michael Gothard in the Rape of Christ scene) but are only in the one shot.

During the shoot, stories were leaked to the press — allegedly by a crew member whose wife was playing a nun — about unrest among the cast, orgies and extras leaving the set in tears. "It got nasty and some of the crowd tried to touch the girls up," remembered Sutton. "One of the actresses got a union thing organized; a kind of Mary Whitehouse figure emerged in the middle of it. The one nun who never took her clothes off tried to organize everybody against Ken."

Fleet Street had a field day with the rumors. Indignant headlines like "Devils Brew Is Bitter," "To *The Devils* with This Repulsive Film" and "What *The Devils* Going On?" started to appear. One salacious header even suggested orgies on the set. "I had to sit on a big bed," the headline screamed. "The nuns all around were completely naked. Then two nuns jumped on the bed . . ."

"You'd think the plague had broken out or something," said Sutton. "The newspapers went crazy about it. Photographs and double-page spreads all over the paper."

The old maxim that any publicity is good publicity may not hold true in this case, according to Sutton. "[The early coverage] put an awful lot of people off seeing the film," he said. "In fact, a lot of people didn't go to it. 'We don't go to that kind of film.' They didn't know what it was."

"The part I played was this rather chaste girl, Madeleine de Brou," remembered Gemma Jones. "I used to arrive on set finding everyone in a state of jitters having had to do ghastly things with candles and scary things with their shaved heads and everything but all the girls who consented to shave their heads and be nuns and things wanted to please Ken Russell because it all seemed very exciting. So it was only after the event that people got rather distressed at what they had to do. But I think at the time everybody threw themselves into it.

"It was very intense," she continued, suggesting the atmosphere on set wasn't as dark as has been reported. "I was a very serious young actress so I got myself wound up into a state in order to weep and wail, but I remember it feeling quite safe to do that on the set.

"I remember it with pleasure, although some people you talk to may remember it with horror. I had a good time doing it. I found it very exciting. We had two or three night shoots, which are hell because you just have to keep awake, but there was a lot of hilarity in the caravans. A lot of the actors knew one another from the theater and there was great camaraderie on the set. In fact there is more camaraderie if things are difficult and having to stay up all night and do fairly horrific things . . . there's a certain excitement in that as well."

Sutton remembered the excitement being tinged with tension. "It's a bit like being in Nazi Germany or Soviet Russia," he said. "Everybody starts nitpicking. Everybody gets suspicious. Who's ringing up the newspapers? There's always some sort of dirt hanging near, but it shouldn't have been there. There was a pall over the set some of the time."

"It was pretty gory," Russell told Rex Reed, "but they knew what they were getting into. I never force my actors into doing anything they don't want to do, but English extras are the lowest form of animal, the dregs of the underworld, and they manhandled the girls a bit harshly, and the whole orgy scene got out of hand. Some of the electricians were running off the set from nausea. Then Actors' Equity got into it and there was a fracas in the papers. But the actors love me."

Judith Paris agreed, to a point. "It should not have happened, and I know I sound prissy and English. Where are the boundaries? Where does it stop being art and start being pornography? I wasn't meaning visually, from what you see, pornographic, I mean actually being involved. How much longer can I convince myself that this is a great film director doing high art, or is this a man who has lost his sense?

Somewhere he lost a sense of reality and is allowing things to happen on his film which are pornographic.

"It's very carved into my mind, even now. I feel disloyal talking about Ken in this way because my admiration for him as a filmmaker knows no bounds. But am I speaking the truth here? Yes, I am. For me, it became a very hard thing to do."

"May I say, for all of us," said Melvin, "when you go back and think, this is 1970. Legitimate actors in those days did not do masturbatory shots in the roof. Many of the actors and actresses did things for Ken that you wouldn't have contemplated doing for anybody else. But you did it for Ken because his way of working, his way of describing, his way of using you, you went along with. And you would do anything for him."

"I was a dancer," said Paris. "Dancers have different attitudes to actors. Dancers on the whole do not talk very much. They dance. Actors talk. They talk the hind legs off donkeys, really. It is assumed that a dancer works under orders, rather like a soldier. That was the discipline I learned at the Royal Ballet School and in the company. You shut up and get on with it and the blood is coming through the shoes but you don't stop because that is how life is. Actors will argue and talk and discuss but I had no knowledge of that. So I came to Ken and he'd say jump and I'd jump. And because he was so wonderful and I suppose I was a bit in love with him . . . he was very charismatic. I was young and I knew he was a genius and you go along, but on *The Devils* I reached my Waterloo. Have you ever tried writhing sexually for ten hours at a time? Try it one day. It's not easy."

On a more serious note, she recalled discussing the shoot with actress Dorothy Tutin who had played Sister Jeanne for the RSC in Stratford and in London. "She was very circumspect about it," Paris said. "She said, 'How did you manage?' I said, 'Well, we were on the film for about ten weeks. Every day for ten weeks.' We were on a great deal of the time. I said, 'I think I learned that there are two subjects that it's unhealthy for actors to be involved with over a period of time. One of them is possession and the other one is madness.' I suppose both really bring the two separate faces of the same coin really, but to enact possession over and over and over again, five days a week, six days a week from nine o'clock in the morning to five o'clock in the evening you do start to get a little strange in your behavior. I was coming home and sitting in the bath with a loofah trying to rub myself clean. I was quite disturbed by the whole thing simply because of the length of the filming period, you know?"

Paris credited one of her co-stars with getting her through a difficult scene. "I had to masturbate that candle. Murray Melvin did not help, actually," she laughed. "He was up there in the gallery sending me up rotten doing that. It made me laugh actually. It got me through it. Ken had been aware that Sister Agnes had been hiding behind certain pillars for far too long in this movie and he said, 'Today's your big day. This is your big shot.' And he made me do that, and I did it. I did it."

The disturbing experiences — trouble with his wife, the studio, extras — were starting to take their cumulative effect on the director. "I remember he was a lot easier to deal with before lunch than afterward," said Sutton.

"He should not drink in the middle of the day," added Paris. "Bless him, but he likes his red wine."

"You get a lot of those film directors with huge egos, which certainly Ken had," Sutton continued, "they come on at the beginning of a film full of enthusiasm. They usually wear funny hats and they're leaping about, full of joy and then one day they come in without the hat. You know the shit has hit the fan.

"In his case Warner Brothers were on to him, and he'd start getting a little pissed at lunchtime. I only had one major row with him. It was about him spraying some anti-flare on my armor. Not him doing it, a young boy, the focus puller doing it. Ken came off lunch and started screaming at this guy. 'Who told you to do this?!' It was just one of those silly, too much wine at lunchtime blasts. He just blasted this boy for ten minutes. The rest of the crew all looked the other way. Union solidarity goes quickly out the window when directors start.

"Then he said, 'Right, let's get on,' and I said, 'No, my theater is in front of your camera and you've just shat all over my theater. So I shall return to my dressing room and when you've cleaned it up, call for me.' He howled and complained and I just walked off. I tried to walk off with dignity but it's quite difficult to walk off in a huff in high lifted boots. Walking down three steps and trying to walk off with dignity. I went to my dressing room and waited for it all to cool down."

Despite their occasional disagreements Sutton said, "Even the struggles we had with Ken were fun. There was one enormous scene in the cathedral. I knew very well that because of the politics of the story I had to be seen. But I was way on the far side of the cathedral, away from his camera. I knew that because of the big crowd between me and the camera they couldn't see Baron de Laubardemont and they had to. So I got the props guys to make up a sign and I painted on it, 'Dudley Sutton as Baron de Laubardemont, Representative Fraser & Dunlop, 91 Regent Street London. Here' with an arrow pointing down and I held it up. He looked through his lens. 'What the fucking hell is that! Ha, ha, ha. You bastard!' That was the kind of thing I loved about him."

Bradsell suggested that the atmosphere on set was a direct reflection of the heavy subject matter. "Day after day with this sort of harrowing material," he said, "we all had to keep our spirits up by making the odd tasteless joke or something, and I gather on the set they were always laughing and joking, playing practical jokes to relieve the tension before the next onslaught."

Through all the ups and downs the flamboyant director remained an eccentric sight on set, resplendent in his Donald Duck hat and gesticulating wildly, a habit, according to Derek Jarman, that cost him dearly.

On the day of the shoot of the destruction of Loudun, with a planned explosion that would bring the white tiled walls tumbling down, a misunderstanding put the production behind by ten days.

"I'm not having this fucked up," said Russell, who was described by Jarman as "very moody." To ensure he got the shot, Russell was determined to shoot the sequence himself. Climbing aboard the camera he was yelling directions, waving his hands in the air.

The crew, misunderstanding his hand signals, thought he wanted the explosion triggered immediately. Someone hit the switch and the entire town was reduced to rubble and dust, as Jarman said, "the camera stood idle" and "everyone stood around dumbfounded" by the enormous explosion. The next week and a half of production was spent rebuilding, so they could blow it up again . . . this time with the camera rolling.

Sutton, who is in the scene, remembered it differently. "Memory is tricky," he said. "Everybody remembers things differently but who's to deny my memory of something?"

The explosion was meant to happen after Sutton stepped in front of the camera and nodded, but, said Sutton, "he blew it up before I had nodded. This is how I remember it. I was actually on the set. My memory is that people were so fed up with Ken by then, at his rages, that nobody was volunteering to press this button, so he said, 'All right, I'll bloody well do it,' and he goes, 'Action,' and just before I step in front of the camera — there's a big Panavision lens — and just as I'm stepping into the camera, he presses the button before I have even arrived and nodded. To my memory that's what happened. Then we had to come back a month later and shoot it again.

"We all hooted with laughter. We were absolutely thrilled because he'd been such a bastard. It was terribly funny and I don't think he ultimately minded. He didn't mind charging Warner Brothers another forty K or whatever it was to build another wall. Part of the joy of him was him rebelling against the studios, the money boys."

With the set in ruins it was time to shoot the final sequence in the film. Gemma Jones, who described herself as "inexperienced" and "green" during the shoot, learned how hands-on Russell could be. In the film's final scene, Madeleine de Brou, the film's only truly sympathetic character, watches as her husband's ashes are spread to the four winds. She walks through the rubble of Loudun and, finding a gap in the flattened walls, exits, on her way to starting a new life or, at the very least, leaving the old one behind. Against that bleak image, the credits roll.

"I remember coming on to the set that morning and Ken Russell said I didn't look grubby enough and I was sent back to the makeup caravan to break me down a little bit and make me a bit more grubby," she said. "Then I came back on the set again and he said I still wasn't grubby enough. So he put his hand inside the canteen where we'd had our bacon sandwiches and took a great lump of grease out and rubbed it into my hair."

According to Russell's fourth wife, Lisi Tribble, the shot of Madeleine walking over a hill of broken bricks, surrounded by the ghostly images of Protestant corpses hanging on posts, inspired Roman Polanski's final scene of his Academy Award–winning *The Pianist*.

The shoot had been long and grueling, taking its toll on everyone involved. Russell and Reed were barely on speaking terms by the end. According to *Evil Spirits* author Cliff Goodwin, the pair "could not bear to be in the same room. There was an emptiness in the relationship which needed to 'lie fallow' until it recharged."

"I think we all got insane," said Judith Paris. "I used to watch Ken. I knew him so well. Ken came into his own on a small shoot where he had the cameraman of his choice, the sound recordist of his choice, a trusted PA and very often his wife doing the costumes and a group of trusted actors he knew. All friends. He didn't care if you had an Equity contract or if you were a member of a union or not. His creative juices were extraordinary on his small-scale films. I used to watch him on *The Devils* surrounded by the panoply of a kind of massive production thinking, 'How do you see your way through this? How do you see your way round this with thousands of people?' Sometimes I thought he was losing what he was so good at."

Who knew the worst was yet to come?

Chapter Six

THE DEVILS' CONTEXT

"You will scream! You will blaspheme!"
— Father Barre

July 1971 was filled with historical events that would change the pop culture and political landscape forever:

- Jim Morrison dies in Paris aged 27
- Richard Nixon lowers the voting age from 21 to 18
- The United Kingdom increases its troops in Northern Ireland to 11,000
- The South Tower of the World Trade Center is finished, topping out at 1,362 feet
- Corey Feldman is born in Chatsworth, California
- *The Devils* premieres in the U.K. and U.S.A., the second of three X-rated films to be released by Warner Brothers in a twelve-month stretch (between *Performance* and *A Clockwork Orange*)

In finding a context for the release of *The Devils* it's useful to place the film alongside 1971's other major movies. The year's top ten box office was bookended by decidedly family-friendly films — *Fiddler on the Roof* was the box office champ with a gross of $38,261,000, while the Disney musical *Bedknobs and Broomsticks* brought in $11,426,000 to come in at number ten — but it's the movies in between that really tell the tale of how the cinema was changing in the early part of that decade.

"This was around the time of *O Lucky Man!* and

Clockwork Orange and the late release of *Performance*," explains *Sid & Nancy* director Alex Cox. "There were some very good British films coming out then, pushing back all the barriers of narrative and 'good' taste. . . ironically all paid for by Americans!"

The year's second-highest-grossing film, *The French Connection* ($32,500,000), is decidedly not a kid flick. Instead it's a gritty, alienating study of human nature starring Gene Hackman as Popeye Doyle, a hot-tempered New York City narcotics cop. Steeped in Nixon-era paranoia, it played with the idea that the good guys didn't always play by the rules. The film netted Hackman a Best Actor Academy Award (along with Best Director for William Friedkin and a Best Picture statue) for his portrayal of Doyle as an anti-hero, a racist, mean-spirited cop who bends the rules when necessary.

Further down the list at number five is *Dirty Harry* ($19,727,000), a crowd-pleasing critical hit that set the template for "loose-cannon" cop movies (if not for this film Mel Gibson and Bruce Willis might have spent their careers playing pretty-boy beat cops). As the .44 Magnum–toting cop Clint Eastwood indelibly etched "Dirty" Harry Callahan into cinematic consciousness, putting the words, "'Do I feel lucky?' Well do ya, punk?" on everyone's lips.

Like Doyle, Callahan was a wild-card cop who nonetheless got results, a hero for people who felt the authorities were losing the battle against crime. It was a zeitgeisty message that hit home, particularly to urban audiences.

In terms of framing the release of *The Devils*, however, two films loom larger than the rest. One made the U.S. Top Box Office list, while the other, bogged down by censorship and controversy, narrowly missed.

Like *The Devils*, Stanley Kubrick's *A Clockwork Orange* (number seven on the top ten grossers of the year with $17,000,000) and Sam Peckinpah's *Straw Dogs* both contained cerebral social commentary presented in very shocking ways. Both movies similarly ignited firestorms of controversy. Kubrick's and Peckinpah's films were noted — and endlessly debated — for their unique depictions of violence.

A Clockwork Orange, based on the 1962 Anthony Burgess novel of the same name, is set in the near future in a totalitarian Britain. Gang leader Alex (Malcolm McDowell) and his droogs, Pete, Georgie and Dim, indulge in Alex's twin pleasures, Beethoven and ultra-violence, until Alex is captured and rehabilitated with a controversial psychological conditioning technique.

Kubrick spares nothing in his portrayal of the droog violence. Alex and company are sneering, sadistic punks without a trace of humanity. Bad men had been portrayed on-screen before, but the film's level of brutality broke new ground. Called "ice cold" and "indecent" by one writer and "a paranoid right-wing fantasy masquerading as an Orwellian warning" by Roger Ebert, the movie isn't for the weak of heart. In one brutal scene Alex tap-dances his way through an attack on a helpless victim while "Singin' in the Rain" bops along on the soundtrack. It's a mocking serenade to the action, but the violence isn't simply played for titillation or exploitation.

Kubrick calibrates the shocking scenes with social commentary about the state of society and free will. Like all great genre films, *A Clockwork Orange* isn't just about what you see, it's about the ideas and the reasons for what you see on-screen.

Writing in *Saturday Review* Kubrick described the film as "[a] social satire dealing with the question of whether behavioral psychology and psychological conditioning are dangerous new weapons for a totalitarian government to use to impose vast controls on its citizens and turn them into little more than robots."

The horrific, dehumanizing ultra-violence of *A Clockwork Orange* earned the film an X in its original release (later Kubrick swapped thirty seconds of sexually explicit footage for less incendiary shots for the R-rated 1973 re-release) from the MPAA (Motion Picture Association of America). The United States Conference of Catholic Bishops' Office for Film and Broadcasting, citing the film's mix of sex and violence, branded it with a C (Condemned) rating (later adjusted to an O — Morally Offensive — when the C rating was abolished in 1982).

In the United Kingdom the reaction was even more extreme. Not only was *A Clockwork Orange* given the expected X rating but there were also legal claims that the movie inspired copycat crimes. In the 1972 trial of a boy from Bletchley accused of killing a younger child while wearing Alex's uniform of white overalls, black bowler hat and combat boots, defense counsel announced "the link between this crime and sensational literature, particularly *A Clockwork Orange*, is established beyond reasonable doubt." In another case a rapist allegedly sang "Singin' in the Rain" during the commission of his crime.

So many gallons of ink were spilled on these stories, linking Kubrick's Best Picture–nominated film to real-life violence, that Anthony Burgess suggested that the film might be too effective. He said the film was "brilliant," so brilliant that it might be dangerous. He added that Kubrick had made "a film which seemed to glorify sex and violence."

The film didn't simply create controversy, but hostility as well. Ultimately Kubrick self-censored the film, withdrawing the movie from release in 1973. After his death his widow, Christiane, explained the reason for the director's decision wasn't related to the copycat crimes, but that he and his family had received several death threats because of the film. The movie remained unseen in Great Britain until 2000 when it was re-released with an 18 rating.

Editor Michael Bradsell found some irony in the BBFC's treatment of *The Devils* versus that of *A Clockwork Orange*. "I was rather surprised to find out recently that the same examiners who found [*The Devils*] so horrifying loved the director's cut of *A Clockwork Orange*, which I have great difficulty with myself. I find it to be a cold calculating picture in which the violence, to my mind, is often gratuitous. The violence and alleged blasphemy in *The Devils* was always to make an important point in the story. I suppose you could say it is a question of degree. Do you need one layer of violence to explain [the story], or do you need two? Whether it is one layer or two, I think it is an important inclusion in [*The Devils*'] important story."

Another popular film that year also raised hackles. Critic doyenne Pauline Kael labeled *Straw Dogs* a "fascist work of art" in part because of its violence against women, in part because of its dim view of pacifism. Dustin Hoffman (who says he's not a fan of violent films and only took the role for the money) plays David Sumner, a mild-mannered American mathematician who relocates with his wife Amy (Susan George) to an isolated English village. Soon they become the target of harassment from the locals and the veneer of their new pastoral life is stripped away to reveal savagery. The film climaxes in a bloody confrontation that tests Sumner's manhood.

Because of its steroidal portrayal of violence and two brutal rapes, *Straw Dogs* was given an X rating by the British Board of Film Censors and only earned an R rating in the U.S. after the studio edited the first rape scene. The advent of video gave the BBFC another chance to censor the film, banning it from being released on video or DVD from 1984 until 2002.

Once again *Straw Dogs* fell foul of censors unable to look beyond the violence. The rape scenes are without a doubt brutal and unpleasant, but, like the violence in *A Clockwork Orange*, aren't libidinous or the subjects of fetish. Instead they push the audience to reexamine the savage nature of man. Are they unpleasant? You bet. Are they brutal? Absolutely. But that's the point, and Peckinpah makes it with the subtlety of a sledgehammer to the side of the face.

"If you look at a movie like *Straw Dogs*, which was heavily influenced by a book called *The Territorial Imperative*," said director Rod Lurie, who in 2011 directed a big-screen remake of the 1971 classic, "Peckinpah seems to be saying that violence is in the genetics of all men and therefore we must be aware of it so we can control it. It was extremely fascist thinking but that also seems to be the thing with *Dirty Harry*.

"*A Clockwork Orange* is a much more clinical look at that but I think artists were trying to provide the answers to what society was asking then. It was a very, very violent era. There is violence in *The Devils* but it is obviously a much more sexual film than anything else. My feeling with that film always has been that the hedonism is not mutually exclusive to civilization or civility. It is, in fact, the different side of the same coin."

As in similarly themed films of the era like *I Spit on Your Grave*, the violence in *Straw Dogs* isn't stylized and that's what makes it so disturbing. Granted *I Spit on Your Grave* has a much more enlightened approach to female sexuality — the victim-turned-vigilante is a strong woman who is attacked because she is confident and successful — but *Straw Dogs* has a deeper more complex meaning. It's

Peckinpah's most multifaceted look at his lifelong obsession — masculinity in all its forms — shining a light on Sumner's intellectualism, suggesting that by retreating into a haze of academia he opened the door to the real world and all its hazards.

"Far from being a 'fascist' film," wrote critic Colin Polonowski, "*Straw Dogs* is a wake-up call to the disengaged and the unaffected that the world outside can't be forgotten." That was a potent message in the Vietnam era.

"This was an era in which people were searching for answers to the madness that was going on around them," said Lurie, "and filmmakers were trying to provide some of the answers. You had everything from the assassinations of Kennedy and King to Vietnam to the Whitman murders to My Lai. I think all of society was trying to understand how human beings could do such things."

The movies that came to define that era were often violent allegories. Another Peckinpah film, which was praised and condemned in equal measure for its violence, had an impact on Joe Dante. "I remember watching *The Wild Bunch* for the first time," adds *Gremlins* and *The 'Burbs* director Dante of the period. "It was obviously about Vietnam. When we went to these movies we were already radicalized by the Chicago Convention. People who weren't even political had suddenly become very political and also they were being drafted so there was a general air of anti-authoritarianism on people my age to begin with and *The Devils* was nothing if not the ultimate anti-authority movie."

These four films pushed the boundaries of on-screen violence in ways that Ken Russell wouldn't have even considered. None are passive films. Each brims with the obsessions of their makers, and for that each was the subject of controversy and censorship; that much they have in common with *The Devils*. Where the main offenders differ, however, is that eventually they became accepted by the mainstream. *Straw Dogs* was remade with an all-star cast by director Rod Lurie in 2011 and *A Clockwork Orange* has become a cultural touchstone, with everyone from Lady Gaga to David Bowie to Kylie Minogue, who dressed in a black bowler hat and a white jumpsuit on tour in 2002, paying tribute. It was even played at the Cannes Film Festival and released on Blu-ray to mark its fortieth anniversary. And yet *The Devils* remains unseen.

Perhaps it's because the other films didn't mix religion and violence. That was up to Russell, the only filmmaker, film critic Chris Alexander says, who could have made *The Devils*. "I'm trying to sort this metaphor out now and it's going to be clumsy," he said, "but it's like a twelve-year-old kid who's picking his nose and farting and everything else. He's rude but underneath it all he's a fucking genius and if you really pay attention to him instead of being shocked by all his exterior jumping jacks, underneath there really is something that is brilliant. I think that's why *The Devils* isolated people the way it did at the beginning. You know, the smash cuts to the maggots involve you and engage you on a certain level and then kick you in the balls in the next frame. It's a challenge to any kind of pedestrian audience to keep up with Russell. I don't even know if he is even aware of that but that is just by his nature who he is. That's why *The Devils* is such a pure work of him."

In one respect *The Devils* was birthed at exactly the right time. By 1970, when the film went into serious preproduction, the studio system in America was in tatters. Hollywood was changing, youth culture was king and the studios were desperate to cultivate new, hip talent to churn out cutting edge movies to appeal to a younger audience. Ken Russell was an obvious choice. He was talented, had a track record and was outrageous enough to appeal to this burgeoning new audience the majors were so anxious to attract, but competent enough to handle a budget and bring a movie in on time.

"You have to remember what the environment was at the time," says Joe Dante. "In 1969 *Easy Rider* had come out and knocked all the business into a cocked hat. Studios were concerned they didn't know who their audience was, and so they went and made a lot of pictures they thought were aimed at an audience that only American International [Pictures] had been exploiting and now suddenly it was mainstream. Do you think a movie like *Alex in Wonderland* [director Paul Mazursky's bizarro 1970 slice of Hollywood ephemera that was called "a pretentious imitation of the seminal *8½*" by one critic] could have ever been made if it weren't for the fact that they didn't know what to make?

"I started making films in the '70s. Before that I was working for [Roger] Corman, we were cutting trailers and making exploitation films and I can tell you there has never been a period like the seventies. For one thing the ratings system had come in and you were now allowed to show things you never could have shown even ten years earlier. So the early '70s is one of the most astounding periods for film and not just in America but worldwide because it was the pre-blockbuster age. That all died when *Jaws* and *Star Wars* came out and all of a sudden movies were different, they were corporate behemoth movies and obviously aimed at a very specific audience of young people, whereas by the time *The Devils* came out there was still a very polyglot audience of different ages who were looking for something different, something interesting and because of the experimentation that was going on at the studio level you saw films made that never would have been made before then."

It was perfect timing for this cutting edge kind of film-making. While a nunsploitation movie never would have been green-lit by anyone on the left coast in less frantic times, it fit the mold of what Hollywood was looking for at the time, except that Russell was years ahead in his thinking. Depictions of the devil and possession weren't unheard of on the big screen before 1971, but for the most part were less provocative than the images that sprang from the director's imagination by way of the pages of history.

The first film images of the devil appeared as early as 1896 in a three-and-a-quarter minute French short called *The House of the Devil*, and exorcisms were depicted on screens as far back as 1912. Filmed on location in the Holy Land, *From the Manger to the Cross* features Jesus "healing a demoniac," a scene that earned great notoriety and made the film one of the highest grossing movies of its day. More dramatic was the opening scene of Cecil B. De Mille's 1927 silent epic *The King of Kings* — described by writer Charles Musser as "the silent screen's most elaborate realization of 'the greatest story ever told'" — where Jesus confronts the seven demons inhabiting Mary Magdalene. It's a stunning scene, complete with special effects showing the wraithlike evil spirits swirling around as they are cast out.

According to Father Peter Malone of the Missionaries of the Sacred Heart order, these images, and others, "are the staple of these 'Jesus movies' and have inserted themselves into the popular as well as the Christian imagination." In fact, throughout the studio era, images of exorcism were rare and almost 100% were confined to "Jesus movies." Satanic cults and Old Scratch himself were often name checked in movies like *The Seventh Victim* and *Beat the Devil* but little if any effort was usually made to cast them out.

By the end of the 1960s, the most tumultuous decade of the twentieth century, the studio system was in tatters and with that fraying came a more permissive attitude toward depictions of religion on-screen.

Rosemary's Baby, Roman Polanski's 1968 classic tale of paranoia and Satanism, not only contained ideas — Mia Farrow giving birth to the son of Satan! — that would have made old-time studio head Jack Warner turn in his grave, it also showed Farrow leafing through the Easter 1966 issue of *Time* magazine featuring the cover headline "Is God Dead?"

Never before would such a question have been asked, and more tellingly, never before would the question have gone unanswered. After all, the movie ends with (spoiler) Farrow gently rocking her new devil baby to sleep, as evil seems to have triumphed over good. Diabolically popular — it was celebrated by many critics and nominated for two Oscars (winning one for Best Actress in a Supporting Role for Ruth Gordon) — *Rosemary's Baby* ushered in the devil's epoch on film.

Of course the most famous devil movie of the 1970s, *The Exorcist*, wouldn't arrive until 1973, but in those days the pace of popular culture was much slower. Today trends come and go at the speed of light, but even though there is a five-year lag in the release dates of Polanski's film and the story of Regan MacNeil's dance with the devil, a direct link can be drawn between the two.

Both are based on books that, as author Stephen King said, were "written and published at the time the God-is-dead tempest was whirling around in the teapot of the 1960s" and both, while played as horror films, are actually brooding meditations on faith. There may be evil, they suggest, but if this evil exists, then so must the good which combats it. Both are dark movies, but neither is cynical.

It was into this atmosphere — set to a soundtrack of "Sympathy for the Devil," which was released in 1969 — that *The Devils* was birthed and the timing may explain why critics were so blindsided by Russell's vision. The fiendish themes of *Rosemary's Baby* and *The Exorcist* were one thing, but Russell took a different approach and, in Huxley's words, transformed "the would-be sublime into the comic, the downright farcical." Otherwise it is difficult to explain why *The Devils* was crucified by critics as a "hideous pantomime" and "a degenerate and despicable piece of art" when, just twenty-four months later, a possessed fourteen-year-old girl would masturbate with a cross, shouting "Let Jesus fuck you, let Jesus fuck you," to mostly rapturous reviews.

In fact, in many ways *The Devils* set the template for *The Exorcist*'s portrayal of possession. Vomiting, check. Crazy possessed spider walking, check. Even the religious masturbation was pioneered by Russell. Black Hole Reviews wrote, "In *The Devils* there's a dozen naked nuns, a statue of Christ, and one very popular church candle." Both are deeply Catholic stories and both are, allegedly, based on true stories. (*The Exorcist* borrows its storyline from a 1949 case of suspected demonic possession.)

So why was *The Exorcist* praised to high heavens just a few years after *The Devils* had been condemned?

Public perception may have shaped the ratings the films received. *The Exorcist* was given an R rating — which, since 1960, has required anyone under the age of seventeen to be accompanied by a parent or adult guardian — without one single cut requested by the MPAA. The rating must have pleased Warner Brothers, who probably expected a box-office-killing X rating based on the film's graphic nature.

"There is no confusion about what kind of film *The Exorcist* is," said MPAA president Jack Valenti. "Much of what might concern some people is not on the screen: it is in the mind and the imagination of the viewer. A film cannot be punished for what people think because all people do not think alike. What might repel and frighten some people might not do the same to others."

Not everyone was on Valenti's side, however. Roger

Ebert, a fan of the film, wondered in print how a film with such graphic special effects could earn that rating. "That it received an R rating," he wrote, "and not the X is stupefying."

Pauline Kael concurred and speculated on why it may have been treated with kid gloves. "If *The Exorcist* had cost under a million or had been made abroad, it would almost certainly be an X film," she wrote in her review. "But when a movie is as expensive as this one, the MPAA ratings board doesn't dare give it an X."

On the other hand *The Devils* was awarded an X certificate in Britain, deeming it "suitable for those aged eighteen and over," a dubious honor it shared with *Plan 9 from Outer Space*, Ed Wood Junior's masterpiece of ineptitude.

Unlike *The Exorcist*, which emerged from its go-round with the ratings board intact, *The Devils* endured a steady stream of indignities before being awarded the British Board of Film Censors' highest grade.

To preemptively placate the Board, Russell snipped away at the film, removing some explicit nudity and trimming the shots of the crushing of Grandier's legs. Bigger cuts, however, were made by Warner Brothers at the same time, including the removal of two particularly disturbing scenes. Still the film received a damning X rating. Make no mistake, however, even in its watered-down form *The Devils* was still an eyeful, a movie that shocked and awed audiences in Britain.

Not surprisingly, even more cuts were demanded stateside. Sister Jeanne's crazed visions and exorcism were toned down as was the film's climax, Grandier's burning at the stake. At the time *Life* magazine speculated that "sex and torture are mere R material, but that the addition of religion as a plot ingredient makes it X."

"I loved Ken Russell's early work," *Exorcist* director William Friedkin says. "I thought some of his later work, like *The Devils*, was over the top and excessive and if the ratings board perceives that that is the case they come down very hard. X means excessive really. A movie may be great, but if it appears to be excessive they'll come down hard on it. If it appears to be part of the story, they're more tolerant. Naked nuns! It's hard to make that part of the story, although you did have the seventeenth-century Devils of Loudun as a reference."

The Devils, and by extension Russell's stance on religion, does appear to be the hook on which opinion hung and this is where the reactions to the two films part ways.

There's no question that *The Exorcist* elicited strong responses from people. Author William Peter Blatty recalls the reaction of one audience member who simply could not watch the spinal tap sequence. "This woman was walking up the aisle with her hand to her head saying 'Jesus. Jesus. Jesus!' I remember thinking I hope that's not [legendary film critic] Pauline Kael!" and H. Robert Honahan of the ABC/Plitt theaters in Berkeley said, "We've had two to five people faint here every day since this picture opened. More men than women pass out, and it usually happens in the evening performance, after the crucifix scene involving masturbation."

Others reacted differently. One man in San Francisco attacked the screen in an effort to kill the demon and Warner Brothers actually hired Father Thomas Bermingham, a priest who acted as clerical adviser on the film as well as appearing in a cameo as the president of Georgetown University, to offer spiritual counsel to audience members overwhelmed by the subject matter.

"I got a call from Warner Brothers asking me to go to Milano," Father Bermingham says, "because they were opening there and they heard that the whole city was in uproar. They wanted to have a psychiatrist and myself present to deal with this. So I flew in and met this Italian psychiatrist — we had dinner and established a good relationship — then we had this lecture which was held in one of the great museums. The lecture was meant to last for forty-five minutes, but after that time nobody wanted to leave."

The publicity fed the public's curiosity and the film lived at the very center of popular culture for most of 1973. *Newsweek* ran a cover story entitled "The Exorcism Frenzy," complete with stories of queasy theatergoers and their *Exorcist* barf bags — Frank Kveton, manager of the United Artists Cinema 150 in Oakbrook, complained, "My janitors are going bananas wiping up the vomit" — as well as the alleged curse that plagued the set and people dying after viewing the movie, making great sensationalist headlines that only drove more box office business. People could not get enough and by year's end the movie was one of the highest grossing (literally) movies of all time.

While audiences couldn't get enough, opinion in religious circles was decidedly mixed. Simultaneously praised as deeply spiritual by the Catholic Church and branded satanic by evangelist Billy Graham, the movie became a flashpoint for debate. Graham suggested that the very celluloid the movie was printed on was somehow evil.

"I have great respect for Billy Graham," said Blatty, "but I thought that was one of the most foolish statements I have ever heard. I would have attributed it to senility except he was only thirty-nine or forty at the time. But to this day I still have no idea what he meant by that. I mean, obviously there is a power in the film to move you, to have a disturbing effect upon the viewer which is greater than the sum of its parts. It's mysterious, yes. But my God, it's not evil."

The Catholic Church endorsed the film — despite Friedkin's assertion that he wasn't "doing a commercial for the Catholic Church," one writer called *The Exorcist* "the biggest recruiting poster the Catholic Church has had since the sunnier days of *Going My Way* and *The Bells of St. Mary's*" — seeing it as something more than simply a horror film. Recently Australian critic Matthew Pejkovic wrote, "One thing is for certain, with the world stepping further away from the Church and into self-annihilation, the role of priests, nuns and laypeople of Catholic faith are more important now than ever. *The Exorcist* is a powerful, if not fantastical, reminder of that." But the film had been banned here and there and even *Christianity Today,* while suggesting that the movie's virtue was that it depicted how severe evil on earth could be, took pains to remind readers of the J.R.R. Tolkien quote, "It is perilous to study too deeply the arts of the Enemy."

If all the reaction to *The Exorcist* was heated and divisive, it was mild by comparison to the response garnered by Russell's film.

"It's probably the way they were handled and the story," Friedkin said when I asked him why *The Devils* was hammered by the censors and his film was not. "*The Exorcist,* in spite of its notoriety, was perceived to be a realistic presentation of real people against a supernatural background. But it was also a popular novel before it was a film and people came to it knowing what to expect. The other thing is, and the main reason, to answer your question, is that the ratings board had changed and become more liberal from the time of *The Devils* to the time of *The Exorcist.*"

Chris Alexander says, "*The Exorcist* is a very safe movie. It's very pro-Catholic and doesn't challenge on the level that *The Devils* does," and critic Mark Kermode thinks *The Devils*, despite its lack of reverence, is an important starting point for a serious look at religion.

"Movies as diverse as Ken Russell's *The Devils*, Martin

Scorsese's *The Last Temptation of Christ*, and even Monty Python's *Life of Brian* have all been branded as blasphemous and attracted sanctimonious calls for bans," he wrote in the *Guardian*, "yet all provided platforms for the serious and heated discussion of issues of faith in an increasingly materialistic, secular society."

Placing aside *The Devils*' demonic tone for a moment reveals a deeply spiritual core. The film, for all its outrageousness, feels like Russell's manifesto on governmental abuse and distortion of religion.

When Grandier speaks up against the exhibition of the mass exorcisms with the words, "You have turned the house of the Lord into a circus, and its servants into clowns. You have perverted the innocent," he — and by extension, Russell — is in the moment, railing against the situation, not the church itself.

Russell maintains the film is a political and not religious film, a feeling seconded by Bradsell. "It is the only film Ken has made that has a strongly political message," he told me in 2011. "I think he himself has said he feels if you make political films of a contemporary nature that politics is such a fickle thing that a couple of years after you've made it, it's already outdated. But he felt he could take a historical subject like this and make a strongly political film."

The truth is that it is both a political and horror film and more. It's part political commentary, part horror film, part nunsploitation and part fantasy. It's such a complex film, so open to interpretation, that likely even Russell doesn't know exactly what his intention was.

Rumor has it that every day on set brought a new analysis from the director on what the film was really trying to say. In the documentary *Hell on Earth* composer Peter Maxwell Davies says, "He's got a mind which darts from one mood to another mood very quickly. From one opinion to another.

I remember him, one day, saying this was a political one, the next day it was a religious film, the next day it was about persecution pure and simple. He would have different attitudes at different times and it changed him."

"He changed his mind all the time," Maxwell Davies told me in a 2011 interview. "Then he just got on with it and realized that this was something that was crystallizing as it was being made in his mind. I think its multidimensionality was occurring to him as they were shooting."

Even Russell's take on the possessions in the film is political rather than profoundly religious. *The Exorcist* treats demonic possession as an actual phenomenon, a scourge which the Catholic Church is able to nullify through prayer and sacrifice. In direct opposition to that position is *The Devils*, which treats the possessions as an offshoot of hysteria, caused by sexual repression and coercion. In Russell's vision the corrupt Church — represented by zealots and fools — uses possession as a tool to intimidate and manipulate the innocent.

Rue Morgue Magazine founder Rodrigo Gudiño said,

> The world definitely was not ready for *The Devils*! But seriously I think the film's differing depictions of the Catholic Church probably went a long way to informing critical reception.
>
> *The Exorcist* was able to excuse open blasphemy on the grounds that, ultimately, it depicted the church in a very favorable light (people still refer to *The Exorcist* as one of the Catholic Church's most effective tracts). *The Devils*, on the other hand, did the exact opposite; it exposed a period in church history that is still a lingering embarrassment. Back in the early '70s the religious right held much more sway than it does now ('twas a time when the Catholic League

of Decency could still get films banned) and even if that grip loosened as the decade progressed, there was still something very relevant and sacred about Christianity in film (think of the success of franchises like *The Omen* and *The Amityville Horror* later in the decade, not to mention popular culture's widespread interest in Christian dispensationalism — from heavy metal to *The Late Great Planet Earth*).

Additionally *The Devils* is a very different type of film; you have Ken Russell's eccentric personality written all over it and, on the whole, it seems like a much more personal work than *The Exorcist* was for Bill Friedkin. So the implication was that Russell's *Devils* amounted to one director's open critique of a religious institution, whereas *The Exorcist* concerned itself with spiritual matters that were still very relevant to a lot of people. Russell was too much too soon, God bless him.

When I asked Alex Cox if he thought a film like *The Devils* could be made today ("No, it could never be made today. British producers don't have the money to try something like it") and if it is a film that only could have been made in Britain ("I imagine the Italians could have done something similar. But probably nowhere else would it have been attempted") his admiration for the film comes through in his concise answers.

When I ask if there is a director out there today who would have the audacity to create a scene like The Rape of Christ, Rod Lurie said, "It's not a question of the filmmaker having the courage. It's the ability to get the financing to do it."

"The movie is so elaborate and looks so expensive," agreed Joe Dante, "that to try and marshal those kind of production forces together to make a picture with that kind of impact, it would have to be funded independently by some crazed millionaire."

Lloyd Kaufman echoes Lurie and Dante. "What's ironic is that today you can show artwork with piss on Jesus. But the big studios, there's no way they would make a movie like *The Devils* today. It would never happen, such a personal statement on such a lavish level. Even *The Passion of the Christ* was made independently and Mel Gibson distributed it independently. If anyone wants proof that the 1970s brought you a freedom of art and expression I would say *The Devils* really shows it."

Chapter Seven

THE FILM'S RELEASE

"My lords, I am innocent of the charges."
— Grandier

Considering the laundry list of troubles Russell and company had to endure once Russell yelled "That's a wrap" on the final day of shooting, editor Michael Bradsell remembers the shooting itself as a relatively stress-free experience.

"Ironically enough, looking back on it, in most departments it was one of the smoothest running productions I can remember in terms of a feature film," he told me. "There weren't any major egotistical tantrums from the cast. Ken, who often had a very short temper, didn't seem to lose it so often. Traditionally one expects problems with major feature films but they didn't come up until the end of producing the director's cut then followed when Warner Brothers found out what it was they'd bought.

"I don't think we saw anybody from Burbank on the set during the shooting. I think a couple of executives came over for the wrap party. It was only when they came over to see the director's cut that the proverbial shit hit the fan. From then on it was quite a nightmare."

Even before its official release, *The Devils* attracted controversy like a flame attracts moths. To brace himself for the expected onslaught, in January 1971 Russell showed an unfinished rough cut of the film to selected test audiences, including BBFC examiner John Trevelyan and director Michael Winner. "When one shoots a controversial scene you always hope for the best," said Russell. "You hope the censor is going to understand and you hope that you can convince him it isn't just for sensation sake, it's an integral part of the truth."

The chief censor used his years of experience with the BBFC to make unofficial suggestions for cuts he was sure the board would demand. "It was a sort of very friendly conversation in which he said, 'Ken, I'm afraid I'm going to cut your throat,'" Russell said to Mark Kermode, imitating Trevelyan, "'er . . . cut your best scene. But don't take it against me because that's my job, lad.'"

Joking aside, Russell admits that Trevelyan understood what the film was — an attempt to portray a historical event in an artistic way — but notes that he also understood that his less progressive colleagues at the board likely would not stand for the film's harsher content.

"Of all the dozens of hours I spent in arguing the pros and cons of this and that with John," said Russell, "only one moment still sticks in my mind. 'I'm afraid we can't have Vanessa saying cunt,' John said. 'It's taken me ten years of fighting just to get [the word] fuck accepted. I'm afraid the British public isn't ready yet for cunt.'"

After seeing the rough cut, director Winner reported to Trevelyan that the Rape of Christ sequence was essential to the film but the censor's hands were tied. It was likely that if the film was released in all its uncut Grand Guignol grandeur it would run afoul of the Obscene Publications Act, originally put in place in 1857 to protect the good citizens of England and Wales from "deprave[d] and corrupt" material. The act cast a wide net covering everything from novels to films, and starting in 2010 even online text chats.

Perhaps the most famous OPA prosecution was the *Lady Chatterley's Lover* obscenity trial in 1960. Although first published in 1928, D.H. Lawrence's last novel was not available in Britain until 1960 when Penguin published an unabridged version, complete with the author's "fucks" and "cunts" in place. Despite chief prosecutor Mervyn Griffith-Jones's opinion that it was not the kind of book "you would wish your wife or servants to read," after a sensational trial a verdict of "not guilty" was returned and the book could legally be sold.

Trevelyan recognized the film was a sitting duck for criminal prosecution and tried to ready Russell for the BBFC's ruling. "I went to one meeting with Trevelyan," Bradsell said in our interview, "but by that stage we'd already had to implement some of the strong suggestions that had been made to Ken from John Trevelyan informally before he had seen it officially. He'd seen certain sequences because he'd been very interested in the film from the script stage. He had to sort of wear two hats. One was the informal, 'Look Ken as a person I would say this. . .' and the other hat where, as the president of the board, he had to say, 'No, the findings are this. We must do this and that.' I think he was as lenient as he felt he could be to Ken because he really liked the film."

A BBFC preview screening in a Mayfair theater yielded predictable results. The Rape of Christ made many of the censors want to wash their eyes out with soap. The scene had to go.

In *Hell on Earth* BBFC examiner Ken Perry, who would serve as deputy director from 1983 to 1988, says, "Although we realized it was a very fine piece of filmmaking we did think, initially, that it might even be rejected because everything appeared to be in excess. I don't think we considered a film from Ken Russell would be rejected but obviously we had to consider all the options."

In a separate interview Perry summed up the general feeling of the board. "It was way over the top," he says. "*Way* over the top. In consequence it was sent backwards and forwards to the board because we don't make the cuts at the board, they're always made by the distributor, and the argument went on for some months.

"You can still establish things according to the original writings on the thing without going into these extreme specifics which I think are probably Ken Russell's more than anyone else's."

"I'm truly surprised that my films shock people," the director said, "and I'm astonished that not everyone could see that *The Devils* was a religious film. There aren't many Catholics in England, but I'm sure that if a Catholic censor had been shown the scene of the nuns and the crucifix, he would have understood what was being said and he would have passed it. Atheist censors are always the ones to be most appalled."

According to Bradsell, the decision to remove the contentious scene was as much the American financiers' as the BBFC.

Bradsell says it was a screening for the studio heads that really put the nail in the film's coffin. "I was involved in a couple of the screenings for the Warner Brothers guys in London," he told me. "One of which I found quite sick-making because we were in a fairly large preview theater and the executives sat down the front and Ken Russell and Roy Baird, the associate producer and I sat at the back. There was a big space between us.

"The executives had got a stenographer who was working a little torch. Even if we couldn't hear what they were saying, or see their body language in the semi-darkness, we knew that every time the torch went on somebody had made a comment that needed to be written down with a view to 'this must be altered or this must be cut out.' The torch went on so early in the film, to our minds there wasn't anything controversial yet, and kept on flashing until it was practically continuous for the last ten minutes. We got so frustrated. There's probably a reason I've never been asked to work on a Warner Brothers picture since.

"Roy Baird turned to Ken and I and whispered, 'Let's get out of here and go have a drink.' We left them to it, which must have been regarded as quite an insult. It's probably as well we weren't there if they'd summed everything they'd written to our faces because when the memo came saying, 'this must go, that must go' it was really quite ludicrous. We got quite apoplectic about it really.

"I gather there was a worse meeting that I wasn't involved in with Ken and Roy Baird like schoolboys summoned to the headmaster for severe punishment or something. They were subjected to quite a grilling about 'why did they perpetrate this disgusting filth onto the public etc., etc. . . .' and Ken was trying very hard to defend it but the more he defended it the worse his attitude became."

Russell said the Americans "really let me have it."

It was apparently at this meeting that the studio executives accused Russell of making a different movie than they had signed up for, a notion dispelled by Bradsell.

"They did apparently complain to Ken that he had not made the film of the script they had been sent for approval, which is 100% not true. Sometimes executives don't have very strong visual imaginations. When I read a script I see a finished film in my head, page by page. Sometimes, if that film actually goes into production that picture might have to change quite considerably, but at least I have a fairly good graphic idea of what the film is going to look like. Particularly if I know the director's other work or if I have worked with him before. But I think these script readers at Warners just took the messages of the setting of a particular scene as something quite perfunctory whereas it was a crucial blueprint for the kind of violence or blasphemy that was going to take place. They couldn't imagine it. The film was an honest and accurate portrayal of what was in the script, they just hadn't had the imagination to see it.

"I feel that if the script readers had got any knowledge of Ken's previous work they would have known what to expect," he continues. "The last BBC film I cut for him was called *Dante's Inferno*, which was a biography of the pre-Raphaelite movement. It starts with a scene of grave robbers opening a grave. You see, by flickering torch light, the rotting corpse of a woman. A hand comes in and retrieves the book of poems that Rossetti had buried with his late wife but later, when he got writer's block, he decided he could do with those poems.

"The image is very strong, quite distasteful I suppose, and that was three or four years before he made *The Devils*. If they'd been watching some of his television films they would know immediately what to expect and maybe at that stage start vetoing things. I suppose for posterity's sake it's better they didn't have the imagination because we got it finished."

There was a fair amount of overlap in the cuts demanded by the studio and those the BBFC required, but both sides also had lists of deletions unique to their organizations. Shockingly Warners went along with all the censors' suggestions and, less shockingly, the BBFC agreed to all of the studio's cuts.

Bradsell says that he and Russell were rocked by the number of changes demanded by the BBFC and the studio.

"We thought the name Ken Russell meant that if we got the money and the go-ahead the studio would accept everything we did. Although I had at the back of my mind that [while] this is really quite strong and controversial if he filmed it it must be okay. It was certainly a shock and a great irritation to me when I found out exactly how strong their objections were."

The full list sent to Russell instructed him to reduce the "elements of gore and violence" during Father Barre's interrogation and subsequent burning at the stake of the Grandier character, drastically alter scenes that "mixed sexual activity and religion in a potentially inflammatory fashion" and trim back the "explicitness and duration" of the film's sexual element, particularly the Rape of Christ sequence and about half a scene with Sister Jeanne masturbating with the charred tibia of Grandier.

Russell tried to play ball with the board, as evinced by a letter he sent to Trevelyan:

Dear John,

I have cleared up the shit on the altar [a reference to Sister Jeanne's shot, but never publicly shown, defecation scene following her Holy Colonic], slashed the whipping and cut the orgy in two. This allows us to achieve several things. The sequence is now much more restrained, no longer self-indulgent and most important of all the rape of Christ concept is strengthened and the idea that true atonement for Christ's sacrifices, the mass, as celebrated by Father Grandier, clarified. I hope you don't feel tempted to tamper with this sequence as it now stands.
Hoping you agree,

Yours, Ken.

P.S. Please show this to Lord Harlech if you think it will have any bearing on his decision.

Lord Harlech was a British diplomat, a pallbearer at President John F. Kennedy's funeral, the founder of HTV and president of the British Board of Film Classification from July 1965 to his death in January 1985. It was his signature that appeared on the ratings that played before the film's opening credits.

After months of letters — in one reply a censor board member wrote, "I have no personal knowledge as to the shape of nuns under their habits, but I doubt they all look like the 'Playmates' of this film." — talks, arguments and horse trading (Russell tried to barter, offering to cut the Soeur Jeanne masturbation scene if the censor would approve the nuns licking the statue of Christ), Russell handed in another version of the film in April which incorporated most of the requested cuts. He heeded the censors' advice and completely removed the Rape of Christ sequence. "They killed the key scene in the movie . . . it was glorious stuff."

"The famous scene that was cut was out of [Warner Brothers'] terror, their fear of displeasing the Roman Catholic Church," chimes in Sutton, "or displeasing middle America."

The movie can function without the scene, and, in fact, has rarely been seen with the sequence intact, but the inclusion of the wild black mass deepens the meaning of the movie. Despite the nudity and obvious sexual component, it is far from titillating. Instead, seen in context, it expertly weaves together the threads of religious, political and sexual corruption into one large, eye-popping tapestry.

"Both Warners and the censor thought it was too strong so I took it out," Russell said. "Short of burning the entire film I had no choice."

In 2011 Bradsell expressed surprise that the heavy pressure to censor the film came from America. "I would have thought the United States, having been born a democracy, was more open minded. I suppose there are some pockets of the U.S. which are not exactly fundamental but have very,

very strong conservative Christian views and if there is a danger of offending them to the extent that the success of the film in financial terms would be jeopardized then even a powerful organization such as Warner Brothers felt they had to be a bit careful. But it was a shock to me."

Not all the requested cuts, however, had the desired effect. "I remember having a long talk with John Trevelyan about the torture scene," said Russell. "They did a particular torture, which was absolutely true, where they put your feet in a metal boot and then drive a wedge between your legs until the bones all cracked. The correspondence on that went on for weeks. I'd cut a bit of the hitting out and he'd say, 'It doesn't look that much different to me.'

"I said, 'Well, I cut half of it out.'

"He said, 'Cut some more out,' so I cut more and in the end there was hardly anything there. He saw it and said, 'It's worse than ever! It's the effect! With just this one hit, it's terrible! Start putting some stuff back in.'"

Trevelyan thought they could pass this version of the movie with an X certificate, a feeling seconded by the board's president, Lord Harlech, who felt the film was a strong and sincere attack on religious hypocrisy.

Unfortunately most of the BBFC examiners weren't of the same libertarian mind and requested four more cuts. Russell made three of the cuts but refused the fourth, claiming it would create major continuity problems in the final product. The board grudgingly agreed and the film was finally cleared for release with an X rating.

Because the edits were almost literally done as a death by a thousand cuts it's hard to determine how much film was actually excised. Estimates range on the low end from four minutes and twenty seconds to eight minutes on the high end. Because they were done gradually the exact amount is lost to time. Also lost to time is any indication of the irony the censors themselves may have felt to be so rigidly enforcing the same kind of code of sexual repression that made possible the sexually explicit exorcisms in seventeenth-century France.

In 1986 James Ferman, then the BBFC's head examiner, said, "I think it is important to say that it was [Lord Harlech] who stopped some examiners with great influence from cutting the film further. He admired the film greatly, he said, 'Russell is a Catholic, he knows his subject, and this film deserves to be shown.'"

But even with the powerful Lord Harlech on his side and without its showcase scene *The Devils* still upset some people. Typical was its premiere at the 1971 Venice Film Festival. Oliver Reed got the day off to a bad start at an afternoon press conference when he suggested opposition to the film was hypocritical. "Why this hypocrisy?" he asked, "Why is it permissible to describe historic events in books and plays, though they must not be shown on the screen?"

The Italian distributors stacked the audience at the Lido Cinema Palace (after the management of the Arean Theatre nixed a public screening for fear of a backlash), inviting everyone from taxi drivers to teenagers, politicians to prostitutes, and of course, church leaders.

The reaction to the film was not surprising.

Dudley Sutton says, "When I worked in Rome, Fellini said to me, '*The Devils!* Aw! Ken Russell!' and kissed his own fingers. In Italy they adored him."

Invited audience members applauded the film; the theologians, not so much. The Vatican's newspaper *L'Osservatore* condemned the film's "perverted marriage of sex, violence and blasphemy" and the Doge of Venice called for a ban on the film.

What happened next was surprising. In protest to the ban a mob burned an effigy of the Doge, which led to an overturn on the ban of Russell's *Women in Love*. Still, *The Devils* was banned. Ironically Russell won the Venice Film Festival's award for Best Director (Foreign Film) that year for a movie that was impossible to see in Italy.

After the ban Reed said, "We were regarded as pornographers in Italy. We'd have been arrested if we went there."

In Britain the worst was yet to come. "Naked nuns," said Russell. "It was enough to send England into a frenzy. A rage." An early, public sign that the studio wasn't 100% on board with the film's content came, of all places, in the movie's press book. This handsome eleven-page pamphlet contained generic articles that exhibitors could plant in local newspapers, ready-made film reviews and ideas for advertising campaigns. It also contained a blurb for a film featurette the studio would make available for promotional purposes.

It's the description of the featurette that raises alarm bells. The first paragraph describes Russell as "a top filmmaker of the era." So far, so good, but it goes on to say, "Most audiences will not appreciate this featurette. Show it to newspapermen, show it to colleges, show it to cinema groups, show it to intellectual and artistic leaders of the community. That's your market for *The Devils'* featurette." The emphatic wording of the paragraph suggests to the exhibitor that they have a hot potato on their hands, with a limited audience. Not exactly what most owners welcome into their theaters. With the studio so unenthusiastic, it's no wonder theaters were wary of the film. The press book might as well have read, "Beware! This movie is not going to be worth your trouble!"

Despite a handful of picketers the London premiere at a Leicester Square theater was lined up around the block. Among those who lined up was future *Repo Man* and *Sid & Nancy* director Alex Cox, then seventeen years old. "I was going to see X-rated films from around the age of thirteen," he says. "Nobody had ID and nobody asked for it." Cox remembers the film had a "controversial reputation," but adds that "films with radical politics and sexual themes were much more common then — and every new Ken Russell film would get the critics talking or complaining or arguing." Asked what his seventeen-year-old reaction was to the film he wrote, "I liked it a lot. Thought it was great."

That was the good news from audiences lucky enough to see the film.

The bad news came over the next few days when some of the most blistering reviews ever given a major filmmaker hit the newspapers. It was as if Russell had insulted the critics' mothers or kicked their dogs, judging by the disdain reviewers heaped on the film. "You would think from the critics' hostility that Ken Russell had tried to pull off some obscene hoax," Reed said.

"I think I was so supportive of the film that I suppose it was naive of me not to have anticipated that kind of reaction," Gemma Jones told me in 2011. "I haven't seen it for years, but I remember when I saw it I was very moved by it and thought it was beautiful and bold and extraordinary. That reaction did surprise me. It seemed very prudish. I was very proud of it."

George Melly in the *Observer* alleged that "instead of contrasting the use of political power with the hideous pantomime it promotes to gain its ends, the whole film is a hymn to sadomasochism. It is vulgar, camp and hysterical." The *Guardian*'s Derek Malcolm dismissed it as a "very bad film indeed."

Even actor John Gielgud threw his two cents in, writing to playwright Hugh Wheeler, "Wasn't *The Devils* awful? I couldn't sit it out."

For Oliver Reed the critical shit-kicking was "water off a duck's back."

Russell was similarly unfazed. "Not one word of criticism written has ever altered in any way my scripts or my next project," he said. "I believe in what I'm doing wholeheartedly, passionately, and what's more, I simply go about my business. I suppose such a thing can be annoying to some people."

Russell answered his critics, who suggested his work was simply self-satisfying voyeurism. "People say, 'Oh, yes, it's all voyeurism and the kick you get out of photographing this stuff.' But it isn't. I mean, you might as well say the same thing about a surgeon. He's got a naked body on his table, and it could be an operation on the vagina. It's just a slab of meat, it's not a person. It's a job you're doing. And there are so many things to get right, like the lighting and the acting and the set dressing, before you come to do the operation. In my case, the film's like that, like a surgical operation. They are planned, not for the effect they are going to have, but for how the story is going to work."

Regardless, it does seem like the review from veteran *Evening Standard* critic Alexander Walker got under his skin.

The two had history. In his pan of *The Music Lovers* Walker declared that if Russell made his proposed biography of Mahler, he would come hunting for the director with an elephant gun. When the two later appeared on BBC's *Film Night* Russell came armed with a large stick which he claimed was his "protection against the threatened assassination."

In a review dated July 22, 1971, Walker called *The Devils* a "garish glossary of sadomasochism . . . a taste for visual sensation that makes scene after scene look like the masturbatory fantasies of a Roman Catholic boyhood."

Sensing a possible showdown between director and critic, a BBC producer for the late-night show *Tonight* (hosted by

Ludovic Kennedy), invited the pair to appear on a late-night news program to hash out their differences. The meeting did not go well. The result was great television — imagine a reality show called *Last Critic Standing* and you get the idea — but didn't mend fences.

Walker hated the movie, actually going so far as to call it "monstrously indecent" on the air. Russell countered by picking apart the review, confronting Walker with two factual errors: reports of scenes that weren't in the film, that were "just figments of his imagination." One was that Russell showed a shot of Reed's penis being crushed. "Well, that may be wishful thinking," Russell said, recalling the incident in a 1996 interview, "but it is simply not in the film!"

When the elaborately coiffured critic — he once tore a strip off a features editor who dared crop out half of his mane of silver-gray hair in a newspaper photo — didn't respond to Russell's satisfaction, the director saw red. "You made it up," Russell sputtered, "didn't you? Admit it. Here's your review!"

As the directed harangued the writer — Russell calls him "old-womanly . . . a carping critic . . . hysterical." Walker noted that Russell actually had a copy of the *Evening Standard* rolled up on his lap. "Rather a large issue that day," he said. "I think about 92 pages."

"I don't make films for the critics!" Russell crowed. "I make films for the public."

In reply to Russell's verbal slap in the face Walker said that if that was true then the public "isn't all that grateful, especially in America," where the film had been doing poorly.

Enraged, Russell bellowed, "Then go to America and write for the fucking Americans," picked up the newspaper from his lap and "bopped [Walker] over the head with his own review and walked off."

It was the bonk heard round, if not exactly the world, at least all around London. The switchboard lit up, not out of concern for Walker, but because Russell had used a four-letter word. The BBC reacted by telling Walker that should he ever appear with Russell on TV again he "must give an undertaking in advance not to provoke him."

The move also made an impression on Walker's colleagues who, for a time, adopted a habit of hitting him on the head with rolled-up magazines and newspapers. "Unfortunately there was not an iron bar in any of them," said Russell. Walker's co-workers even created a verse for the office Christmas panto based on the incident: "We have a little critic / Alexander is his name / Ken Russell bopped his bouffant / But he couldn't dent his fame."

Despite the good-natured ribbing and the indignity to his haircut, Walker walked away from the encounter a changed man. "In fact, I had rather more respect for Ken Russell for forcing his emotions so trenchantly on a critic. The manner of his doing so was, after all, the very embodiment of his filmmaking."

Critics were one thing, but soon more determined foes came out of the woodwork.

The backlash continued, coming now from the Nationwide Festival of Light, a Christian grassroots movement representing the "silent majority" of Britons concerned with society's new permissiveness. Led by filth foe Mary Whitehouse — a middle-aged schoolteacher who thought the BBC was at the center "of a conspiracy to remove the myth of God from the minds of men" and who once forced Top of the Pops to air Chuck Berry's "My Ding-A-Ling" with illustrations to make clear the ding-a-ling was a toy with bells, not a penis — the Festival members called the film "offensive, obscene, repugnant and likely to injure the moral standards of society" and requested that it be banned in small towns outside of London. Many patrons of theaters that continued to play the movie were greeted by makeshift protests from Whitehouse and her followers, complete with sing-along prayer sessions.

When I asked cast members Dudley Sutton and Murray Melvin about the insider's reaction to the trouble Whitehouse was stirring up, Melvin laughed demonically before saying, "One was amused in a way. Sorry for Ken who had to go through all that. You just thought, 'Oh, those ignorant people who don't understand the film and it really is surely very obvious. You don't have to have a Ph.D. to understand it, do you? But they are so bigoted those people, they are so blinded by their catechisms, that they can't see the humanity of that film."

Sutton was equally blunt. "Those idiots," he said. "You've got witch hunts everywhere. People are frightened of ideas. Ken was not frightened of ideas."

Just days after the film opened Whitehouse contacted Dr. Mark Patterson, the chairman of the Greater London Council's film viewing committee, to encourage him to watch the movie. Distressed by the crowds who showed up at the Leicester Square screenings, Whitehouse turned to the GLC knowing full well they could overturn any decision by the BBFC and outright ban the film from London theaters — and as the old saying states, as London goes, so goes the country. Her hope was that a ban in the bellwether city of London would prompt a prohibition nationwide.

Patterson called for a private screening of the movie at County Hall. This was serious business. A handful of disastrous reviews in the newspaper was bad enough but the GLC's involvement was potentially catastrophic. The committee's vote was a squeaker — a sanction was averted by only three votes — but nonetheless, seventeen local councils banned it outright following heavy-handed condemnation by pressure group the National Viewers' and Listeners' Association. (It's been suggested the uproar caused by the GLC's refusal to ban *The Devils* pushed them, a week later, to come down extra hard on the next film submitted to them, *Trash*, presented by Andy Warhol. The movie was refused permission "for the public exhibition of the film in Greater London.")

Trevelyan remained a supporter of the film even though storm clouds were gathering. In his book *What the Censor Saw*, he writes that Whitehouse and company then "began to circularize churches elsewhere encouraging them to protest to their local authorities, and some authorities responded by banning the film."

In a 1996 interview Russell recalled the Festival of Light pickets. "I remember standing outside a cinema, talking to these people and asking them why they hadn't seen it. They were the usual morons, a slightly strange-looking lot, and of course it transpired that they were all acting on instructions from Above."

Terry Gilliam sheds some light on the mind-set of religious activists who protest against filmed art. Following the release of the Monty Python film *Life of Brian* the British comedy troupe found themselves under attack. "As far as being in the center of the controversy I think we all felt proud," he wrote. "We had touched a nerve and hopefully were saying something worth saying. The people who were screaming were the closed-minded bigots and professional organized religiousers that we were aiming at. To have Catholics, Protestants and Jewish groups all protesting without actually seeing the film seemed very ecumenical on our part.

"My mother, a serious churchgoer, had no problem with the film. It was clear to her that we weren't blaspheming since Brian was clearly not Jesus. That's the clear-minded thinking that the ranting mobs on the streets chose not to have."

Russell must have felt under siege in the summer of '71, his *annus horribilis*. While he was busy beating off the critics (occasionally literally) and self-styled advocacy groups in Britain, more trouble awaited overseas.

The reviews the film received in the U.S. redefined the word *vitriolic*, with some even questioning whether or not Russell was stable enough to be trusted with a movie camera.

"Russell's film takes a quantum leap from his abominable *The Music Lovers* into a dung heap," wrote controversial critic John Simon of the *New Leader*. "I shall refrain from saying more because, not having a degree in sanitary engineering, I don't know how to review a cesspool."

The *New Republic*'s Stanley Kaufman sneered, "Russell's swirling multi-colored puddle . . . made me glad that both Huxley and Whiting are dead, so that they are spared this farrago of witless exhibitionism."

Writing in the *Los Angeles Times* Charles Champlin called the film "a degenerate and despicable piece of art," while Judith Crist in *New York* asserted, "we can't recall in our relatively broad experience (four hundred movies a year for perhaps too many years) a fouler film." When Oliver Reed got wind of Crist's review he publicly challenged her to a televised debate, but, perhaps fearing a bop on the head — or worse from the volatile actor — she didn't respond.

Despite their name, the small press magazine *Iconoclast* was aghast at the film, saying it had "all the taste and restraint of a three-day gang bang," and a publication called *Harry in Baltimore* bizarrely labeled it "Goebbels in drag."

Some even went beyond mere criticism of the film to wonder aloud why Russell would make the film at all.

"Even if the characters did exist and the behavior and times depicted are true," wrote Ann Guarino of the *Daily News*, "to what purpose does one exploit a couple of rotten pages of history? It's like opening up a can of worms."

Newsweek even suggested that Russell has "gone beyond extravagance to insanity."

By comparison, *Variety*'s review seemed almost kind. "As if the story weren't bizarre enough, Russell has spared nothing in hyping the historic events by stressing the grisly at the expense of dramatic unity."

According to Pauline Kael at the *New Yorker*, "Ken Russell doesn't report hysteria, he markets it."

More subtle, but just as off-putting, were the ads Warner Brothers took out in several major publications. "*The Devils* is not a film for everyone," screamed the header of a July 19, 1971, quarter-page ad in *New York* magazine. "It is a true story, carefully documented, historically accurate — a serious work by a distinguished filmmaker. As such it is likely to be hailed as a masterpiece by many. But because it is explicit and highly graphic in depicting the bizarre events that occurred in France in 1634, others will find it visually shocking and deeply disturbing.

"We feel a responsibility to alert you to this. It is our hope that *only* the audience that will appreciate *The Devils* will come to see it."

In other words: buyer beware.

"I didn't know about that public health warning," said Michael Bradsell when I read him the advertisement's text. "They were probably a bit worried by the fact that the premiere run in London was picketed by various religious groups. Typically they were people who hadn't seen the film so they could make up their own minds, they just felt instinctively that it was something blasphemous and depraved and so forth and I suppose they thought, if it is like that in

London it could spark riots in the United States."

"This was hot stuff," Joe Dante says of the film and the ads. "[The marketing] guys were not stupid. They didn't go through all those bouts of cutting without realizing there was a lot here to worry about. I think their hope was, based on Russell's reputation and the cast and the fact that it was a quote, class movie, that they would be able to make this work as a commercial picture with a sophisticated audience.

"There was no way they were going to advertise this picture as if it was a German witch-burning movie. They couldn't do it and be Warner Bros., they would have to do what a number of other studios did and just form a sepa-rate company to release the picture. Columbia did that with *Repulsion*, MGM did it with Paul Bartel's *Private Parts* and movies they thought were unbefitting of having their logo on them. If they still wanted to release them they would form another company. But Warners didn't do that. This was a class picture and they were into it for a lot of money and I think they figured this was the best way to protect themselves."

Chris Alexander of *Fangoria* magazine suggests that it wasn't just the nudity and alleged blaspheming that upset sensitive viewers, but something more fundamental, more primal.

"In any movie that has faith or theology at its core there's usually clear-cut lines between right and wrong, good and evil, and I think *The Devils* doesn't have that," he said. "You have to look. You have to force yourself to identify with people who are both good and evil or neither. Grandier is like that. Grandier is our protagonist, our hero, but he ain't no hero. If Grandier existed in contemporary times and was a priest he would be headline news. So we're forced to identify with this guy and I think any time you put an audi-ence, especially one who is Catholic, or religious, and you out this sort of person as your hero, and ask them to sit for ninety minutes and walk sidestep with this character, you're going to get people's backs up immediately.

"Then you throw all that other stuff on top and people are going to be blinded. They're not going to look any further. There comes a point where people just put their blinders up and refuse to search anymore. A guy like Grandier is doing all this stuff, and 'Oh my God, there are no good guys in this movie. He's our hero?' Then you throw the Rape of Christ in there and that's the point of no return."

There were glimmers of hope here and there. After the response of the Catholic Church in Italy and in the U.K. an unlikely ally emerged in the U.S. "Ironically, one of the greatest champions of *The Devils* is the Reverend Gene D. Phillips of the Society of Jesus," Russell wrote in his biography *Altered States*. "He teaches film at Loyola University and was so impressed that he immediately included it in the curriculum."

Later, Russell said that because the movie is taught by Jesuits as if it were a good Catholic film, "chances are, it is."

Critical response, as well, varied in America, differing slightly from the monolith of hate that greeted the film's U.K. debut. *Time*'s Jay Cocks called it "a movie so unsparingly vivid in its imagery, so totally successful in conveying an atmosphere of uncontrolled hysteria that Russell himself seems like a man possessed. Russell lashes his actors into a histrionic verve that is reminiscent in equal parts of the Royal Shakespearean Company, the Living Theatre and Bedlam."

Jonathan Raban of the *New Statesman* praised it as Russell's best film, noting that "reality turns into joke, joke into nightmare," and *New York Times* writer Stephen Farber called it a "visionary work, a prophetic warning of the tenacity of ignorance and superstition."

Despite the handful of good reviews more cuts were required in various U.S. jurisdictions. "There were two versions released in 1971," explains Bradsell. "There was a European version which had about three minutes removed and an American version which had about another two minutes removed which I reluctantly had to deal with. At first I refused to but Ken Russell said, 'They're going to do something anyway, so at least try and deal with it and effect as much damage limitation as you can.' Their requirements were totally inartistic and quite absurd. They had a pathological fear of seeing a female nipple or pudenda on the screen, regardless of the context. It was quite difficult to persuade them that certain things had to remain for purely film grammatical reasons. You can't just start jumping around all over the place."

"It was the incredible shrinking movie," said Joe Dante, who first saw the film at a Philadelphia press screening in 1971 when he worked for *Film Bulletin* magazine. "Every time you saw it something else was missing!"

"They said Mayor Daley of Chicago would get mad if we didn't cut certain things," said Russell, "but I could never see where he fitted in. Then a sales rep from Warners said to me, 'Look here, Ken baby, I've made it with every broad from San Francisco to Timbuktu, but I'm telling you there were things you did in that movie that I wouldn't do to my own mother. We've got to start by cutting out all that pubic hair. Pubic hairs get you an automatic X.'

"'That's very unfortunate,' I said, 'because if we take out all the pubic hair, there won't be much left to the movie, will there?' In the end, my editor made the cuts, and the hairs were strewn all over the studio. And we still got an X rating!"

"Now, an X rating was not a sexual rating," said producer Robert Solo in an interview with Elwy Yost in 1993.

"It was a different X in those days. It got an X rating so they recut the film to get an R rating and having recut the film to get an R rating they released it with the X rating. I never went to see the American version. I was so angry."

The controversy over *The Devils* was not only reported in newspapers and on television. The uproar even made it into the pages of Graham Greene's 1973 novel *The Honorary Consul*, where a Conservative Member of Parliament describes the British entry at a film festival — by some chappy called Russell — as pornographic.

Chapter Eight

RENAISSANCE OF *THE DEVILS*

*"They always spoke of your beauty, and now
I see it with my own eyes and it is true."*
— Sister Jeanne

By the fall of 1971, after months of tussling, controversy and violence (if you count Russell tapping Alex Walker on the head with a newspaper as violence) . . . nothing. The movie was quietly withdrawn from theaters, left tattered and torn, ripped to shreds, literally in pieces for more than twenty-five years.

"At the end of shooting Ken said, 'I'm not going to do another film like that. From now on it's going to be much more gentle, entertaining,' said Bradsell. "Ironically enough, the next film was *The Boy Friend*, which should have been a delight from start to finish but they had horrendous problems both technical and with clashing personalities which made *The Devils* look like a pushover by comparison." *The Boy Friend*, which Russell made later that same year, was a light, fluffy musical.

"Most of my films are reactions from one to another," Russell said. "A merry musical was the surest way to exorcise the misery of *The Devils* we could think of."

And so his Gothic masterpiece was forgotten, save for a further bowdlerized version Warners released theatrically in 1973. Timed to pick up on the spillover publicity *The Exorcist* was generating, the movie — advertised with the tagline "Prepare yourself for *The Exorcist* with *The Devils*" — was a few seconds shorter, shaved of some lesbian allusions and a shot of Grandier's shattered legs. Despite the new version's R rating the film's time had passed and it quietly disappeared until 1981 when Warners released the 1973 print on VHS.

Thus begins the almost impossible to sort out life of *The Devils* on video, DVD and on television. In a 1996 article titled "Cutting the Hell out of *The Devils*," Tim Lucas makes the point that over the years "bastardized edits of *The Devils* have proliferated far and wide," treated to the indignities of pan-and-scan (a method to adjust widescreen images to fit the dimensions of a standard definition 4:3 aspect ratio television screen) and careless unreeling (which will affect the overall run time). "Their individual birthmarks and patrimonies are almost impossible to sort out," he writes.

It is confusing. Home entertainment buffs often cite run times as proof of cuts and distributor interference, but often the differences are simply the result of sloppy video transferring or time compression. For instance, the first U.S. home video release (Warner Brothers Video #11110) reports a length of 105 minutes on the box, but actually only runs 103 minutes. Where did the two minutes of footage go? In short, nowhere. It was time compressed — sped up without affecting the audio — and, if it had been recorded at its proper speed, would actually run 108 minutes, 3 seconds, very close to the original U.S. release running time, but still short of Russell's final cut of 111 minutes.

The British home video release is identical to the U.S. version, despite a listed running time of 103 minutes, 38 seconds. James Ferman, then the BBFC's current head examiner, expressed regret about this version. "To my very great regret it is the American version that is out on video in Britain," he said. "I think it is a great pity. All the nude scenes were cut, most of the sex was cut, the violence was cut down to beyond what we passed in this country. They

[Warner Brothers] were attempting to impose their idea of good taste on this film and really transformed it into a different kind of film. You can't impose good taste on Ken Russell. Russell is Russell and it is a lost cause. You've got to give him his head to some extent, he's a one-off."

Other markets received various versions. The Venezuelan video — titled *Los Demonios* — runs 107 minutes, 50 seconds, but is poorly transferred with a cropped full-screen image and subtitles often blocking the lower third of the image.

The best of the bunch was the Danish VHS. Although poorly letterboxed it featured extra footage and although still incomplete it clocked in at 110 minutes, 7 seconds.

It was the British version that was released as a "deluxe" laser disc in Japan as part of the Ken Russell Collection in 1990. Although presented at the original projection speed — it runs 108 minutes, 3 seconds — it is not letterboxed and with no new scenes there's hardly anything deluxe about this issuing. Worse, it's optically censored. One quick glimpse of pubic hair has been fogged pink as a naked nun sprawls before Duke de Conde.

Television airings are even harder to assess. The now-defunct American pay service ON-TV ran a truncated version of the film in their late-night "For Adults Only" package in 1979–80. A pan-and-scan copy, it frequently blurred as it moved from one side of the screen to the other and, according to film critic Tim Lucas, it was the last time the movie was "shown in America with its original Warner Brothers logo card."

None of these versions, however, contain the film's centerpiece, the infamous Rape of Christ scene.

In 1985 Bravo played a 106-minute time-compressed pan-and-scan version hosted by David Ansen of *Newsweek*, followed ten years later, on May 30, 1995, by a BBC2 screening of the original British theatrical version as part of their Forbidden Weekend series of uncut films. Ironically the BBFC's James Ferman appeared on the broadcast, not to disparage the film, but to praise it. "I rang the BBC when I heard they were planning to broadcast it for the first time just to check it wasn't the American copy they were showing," he told reporter Torin Douglas. The U.S. copy, he said, was "very heavily cut . . . without any respect for the material."

On the show, which commemorated the twenty-fifth anniversary of the film, he stated that if Russell was to deliver the same film to his office today it would likely have passed with no cuts whatsoever.

The Devils could have gone on to be remembered as a notorious film "maudit," or "cursed film," a term created for the Jean Cocteau curated 1949 Festival du Film Maudit in Biarritz, which showcased overlooked and neglected movies — but then something miraculous happened. The film slowly started to worm its way back into the public consciousness.

Fangoria editor Chris Alexander calls the film "the white whale, a hard movie to find," and perhaps that is part of its appeal. The forbidden fruit, hidden from view by Warner Brothers, has a strong lure for film fans.

"All the things that people tell you about the movie are true," Alexander continues, "especially if you see it with the Rape of Christ in it. That shit is offensive and it does provoke and it does rile you and it does offend you, and it does knock you senseless, make you shake your head and smile and say, 'My God, they went there? This got released by a major studio? What? In 1971?'"

The buzz really began in May 1995 when Alex Cox presented the most uncut version of the film (to date) as part of BBC2's Forbidden Cinema weekend. I asked Cox what the reaction to the broadcast was. "I don't know," he replied.

"People are pretty sophisticated and I doubt that anyone except lunatic religious people (like Tony Blair) were upset."

That broadcast was widely bootlegged and later chopped up and placed on YouTube in ten-minute segments, and later in one piece, running a full 108 minutes. Simultaneously a groundswell was fueled by filmmakers and critics like Bryan Singer, Guillermo del Toro and Mark Kermode, who all publicly championed Russell's forgotten masterpiece on Best Of lists.

In 1996 Movieline asked thirty directors to choose a favorite "forget-me-not," an underappreciated film. *The Usual Suspects* director Bryan Singer called *The Devils* "a movie everybody should see. It has some of the best dialogue, characters and subject matter that I have ever seen in a movie. There's a moment when Oliver Reed is being brutally tortured, and they ask him, 'Do you love the church?' His answer, 'Not today.' What a great line. I saw it for the first time five or six years ago on video, and then I saw an uncut print. I've seen it a dozen times. It's an awesome movie that was dismissed by a lot of people — Leonard Maltin gave it 2½ stars in his book."

Later that year English multimedia artist Adam Chodzko created a six-minute film called *From Beyond* reuniting the extras from *The Devils*. *From Beyond* features "a few nuns but I really wanted to work with people who had the most fleeting relationship with the film, as extras, crowd, background etc.," he told me in an email exchange. "I'm very uninterested in the 'stars.' Just those on the periphery!

"I was interested in their participation in a fiction, in order to support that fiction; and what this meant to them in reality. I was also interested because of the long interval of time between the production and this reunion . . . so creating another kind of marginality."

Asked to describe the experience of working on the film

and to try to make sense of it twenty-five years later, the extras — one of them "acted" the role of a corpse — are seen in flashback from the film, writhing around naked, which stands in stark contrast to the mostly middle-aged, straight-laced people they became. *From Beyond* doesn't shed a great deal of light on the shoot, because, as frieze.com suggested, "most of the extras are only able to articulate their experience in terms of chaos." Adds Chodzko, "[There was] a consensus that Russell was very brutal. And the atmosphere was pretty dark and wild!" Nonetheless, it's an interesting look at the much-maligned extras.

In the internet age interest in the film blossomed on DVD and Blu-ray message boards. Facebook has several fan appreciation sites devoted to the film, where passionate discourse is the rule of the day.

"When and if it ever is released we all should steal it and chance being arrested," reads one impassioned message on *The Devils* Appreciation Society Facebook page. "Warner Bros. should not make a cent for their lack of respect for this masterpiece."

The internet and social media have certainly aided a renaissance in interest in the film, but despite offering grainy bootlegs and foggy YouTube footage, they haven't given people the chance to see the movie as Russell intended. That privilege is saved for occasional showings of the film at festivals and rep houses.

Various cuts of the film — some with the Rape of Christ, others without — began screening publicly in the early 2000s.

The film's main angel, ironically, was cut from the same cloth as some of the film's early enemies. Pompadoured BBC film critic Mark Kermode included the movie on a *Sight & Sound* poll of the top ten films of all time and began a renaissance of interest in the film that led to uncovering footage previously thought to be lost. Russell usually has little time for critics; this is, after all, a man whose wife says, "He usually thinks horrible thoughts about his critics," and who claimed responsibility for the death of critic Alexander Walker in print.

"I thought him to death," he said.

Although his brethren had torpedoed the film in its initial release, Kermode is the man most responsible for the film's renaissance. In his book *It's Only a Movie* he describes how a reckless promise to Ken Russell led him down the path to reinstating the supposedly lost footage. "In a moment of rash bravado I told him that I would find that missing sequence and restore it to its rightful place in the film."

In the December 2002 issue of *Sight & Sound*, Kermode continued the story. "It was in the knowledge of its probable destruction that I started searching for this sequence back in 1999, spurred on by Ken's vivid description of the piece and encouraged by recent unearthings such as that of the excised footage from *The Exorcist* . . . Working with director Paul Joyce [whose documentaries on Oshima, Wenders, Roeg and Kubrick had earned great critical respect], I made a nuisance of myself in America, where we enlisted respected archivist Mike Arrick to make ultimately fruitless enquiries at the studio's Burbank vaults. Having drawn a blank, Paul and I turned our attention to the UK, where Ken was now convinced any surviving material would finally have come to rest. Initially the studio was tolerant of our badgerings, particularly since finding extra footage could facilitate a commercially viable reissue of the film."

Bradsell describes Kermode during this period as "rather like a Rottweiler getting hold of somebody's ankle and not letting go. People would check and say, 'No, we haven't got that,' and he'd say, 'Can you look again?'"

Kermode goes on to explain that a final request to check

"one outstanding item which was believed to be utterly innocuous in fact turned up a canister containing negative cuts of whole sequences deleted from *The Devils*."

Bradsell told me he was skeptical at first as to the veracity of Kermode's find. "First of all I thought as nobody except Ken and I would actually know if it was genuine I won't get too excited until I see it for myself," he said.

"Apparently it had been found in a tin in negative form and somebody had very tentatively run a few feet of it on a well-maintained Steenbeck. Then they stopped and told Mark, 'As far as we can see it looks like some naked people dancing around a crucifix.' So he said, 'Don't run any more! That sounds like it. Could you get a print off it?' They did this print and I was invited to Warner Brothers office in London to confirm that was it. Not only was it it but it was in an absolutely pristine state. I'd actually forgotten at what stage we'd removed it but we must have rather confidently gone as far as including it in the assembled negative and having an answer print made with it intact and it was only after they'd seen that that they demanded the removal. It was a section of cut negative that they had removed and stored. One doesn't really run negatives for printing purposes."

Bradsell reinserted those sequences into the film, a job he described as "like time-traveling; like going back to the original color timing at the labs when we released the film initially. I knew it was going to be not particularly complicated but it couldn't just be a straight question of making a cut and opening it up and inserting the new pieces because [originally] we'd done our best to preserve the best of the material which was in the censored area; as much of it as Warners would allow.

"That had to be removed to make for its inclusion in the new section; otherwise you'd be seeing some of the same shots twice. Otherwise it was just a couple of days' work to get it back in. It all came flooding back. I remembered very well what we'd done before. I'd never been involved in anything like that before and it was slightly eerie but very, very satisfying. It was, in a way, as though some unseen hand was guiding me to do justice to what Ken had originally intended."

The time capsule's contents, however, did yield some surprises. "I'd forgotten we'd intercut this sort of obscene orgy with a very simple celebration of mass by Grandier on the roadside on his return from visiting the king," Bradsell said. "Obviously we did that so you don't get three and a half minutes of unadulterated naked orgies going on. Instead you get it into a kind of emotional context. The true celebration of religious mass against this highly politicized frenzy organized by the state. I was, in a way, rather pleased with myself, thinking, 'I can't remember whether that was Ken's idea or mine, but if it was mine, I'm glad I did it.'"

Bradsell also discovered one major omission in the Rape of Christ's restoration. "I couldn't remember whether we had ever recorded Peter Maxwell Davies's music cues for that particular scene," he told me. "Then I remember that we hadn't. I remembered telling him when we were trying to organize a schedule for recording I had to say, 'Sorry Max, I don't know how much you've written for that, or how much time you've spent on it but the orgy is out.' And he pretended to be like a little child who was told Father Christmas doesn't exist. 'No orgy!' he said, and pretended to weep on my shoulder. So we didn't actually record that but there were a couple of other areas in the film with no dialogue where there was a lot of frenzy and rather distraught music and I was just able to copy some sections of that and slot them in in the appropriate areas. As Max's music isn't particularly tuneful anyway you don't immediately think, 'Oh, we've heard that bit before.'"

"We did score that but it seems that's lost," remembers composer Sir Peter Maxwell Davies. "We recorded it. I remember it was pretty wild and wacky. But they had to use something else for that because I think it is gone forever. There were some things which weren't used and things which were cut," he continues, "so I suppose you can just do a switch and it will work out okay."

By the time Bradsell completed the director's cut, however, Kermode says, Warner Brothers' "enthusiasm began to wane."

"Despite offers by Lucida Productions to reinstate this material into *The Devils* at its own cost with the assistance of editor Mike Bradsell," he wrote, "the studio balked, declaring the 'distasteful tonality' of the material to be entirely out of step with current company policy. Once again, the Americans who had initially financed Russell's outlandish vision decreed that the director had gone too far, and chose to censor their own property."

The result, however, was a more complete version than the public had ever seen, a version that had previously only been seen by a very people, and then not since 1971.

"I sort of compare it to other people's director's cuts which either appear on the screen or on television from time to time," said Bradsell, "where the material in terms of the drama is there, but you can definitely see where the new bits have been inserted because they have been cobbled together from various not-first-generation sources. But here, I don't think anyone who wasn't connected to the production would know where the insertions start and stop."

This new rendering was screened to great acclaim at the NFT (National Film Theatre) in London in 2004 as part of their History of Horror series.

The screening was met with a standing ovation and again all seemed primed for an official release. Extras were prepared and the restored print was ready to go until, as Mark Kermode wrote, "in an uncanny echo of their actions in the early seventies, [Warner Brothers] effectively banned the intact movie all over again."

It's rare that a studio takes a second chance to prevent people from seeing one of their movies, but that seemed to be the fate of *The Devils*. Kermode's restored cut now sits on a shelf, gathering dust, despite, as he writes, "having long since been given a clean bill of health by the UK censors."

In the wake of Kermode's restoration several versions of the movie popped up on disc, most of which should come with a buyer beware sticker. For instance, the Euro Cult label release simply used the censored and out-of-print Warners' VHS version as a framework, with some of the previously unavailable scenes sloppily inserted into the action.

Other pan-and-scan versions diminish the beauty of David Watkin's cinematography and Russell's eye for composition.

The best NTSC-format version came in the form of a bootleg from Angel Digital in 2005. The Rape of Christ and other censored footage are reinstated (although the excised torture footage is still missing) to bring it to a running time of 109 minutes, just shy of the original cut's 111. Also included are Mark Kermode's *Hell on Earth* documentary, as well as interviews with Russell, the surviving cast members, censorship activist Mary Whitehouse and a member of the BBFC who participated in the original censorship of the film.

Joe Dante described this version as "a crummy DVD, the one with the documentary on it. It is one of the greatest-looking movies ever made and it is tragic that the only way you can see it uncut is in this awful quality."

The man behind the bootleg, Wayne Maginn, explains how it came to be. "The composite-edit that was given a bootleg DVD-R release was my 'work' (for want of a better word)," he wrote in an email. "I spent years hoping that one day the footage cut from *The Devils* would materialize only to hear several reports over time that Ken Russell and others had all searched for it for many years and with no luck. When Mark Kermode let it be known some years later that he had news regarding the discovery of footage cut from the film I, like many others I am sure, was excited and ecstatic!

"Within a short period of time, it was revealed that a can was found containing much of the cut footage and this would be formed into a documentary for TV broadcast. Unfortunately, I lacked a DVD recorder at that particular time and so had to record the *Hell on Earth* documentary on its original broadcast on VCR. Having purchased a DVD recorder only months later (the desire to back up the documentary on DVD-R being one of the main factors in scraping together the money to finally afford one), I set about cutting together the British X-rated theatrical edit of the film.

"Noting that Mike Bradsell had intercut the restored Rape of Christ scene with footage from the scene with Grandier outdoors, I ensured I removed the shots from the base print I was using so they did not repeat. As closely as I could, I attempted to insert the footage as smoothly as possible with my VCR-to-DVD recorder setup, unfortunately having to trim a few seconds off the opening of the scene where on-screen text appeared in the documentary so as to provide as seamless a transition as possible within my means.

"I felt the film deserved special treatment as far as could be provided and if Warner were not going to then I would do my best to give it some bells and whistles. I just wish I had recorded the documentary on a better format at the time and also had done a better job of the composite. Alas, I lacked the equipment and software that some had at the time!

"Added to a second disc were interview snippets taken from the BBC's *Empire of the Censors* documentary where Russell and others discussed the censorious history of the film and its contentious nature. Former BBFC head James Ferman's intro to the BBC screening was included as I felt he gave due respect to Russell and the film and it was also surprising to hear Britain's strictest film censor speak so highly of the film and its creator. The trailer was ported over from the VHS release, the documentary was from the one and only TV showing it had and the slideshow was assembled from images of materials found online . . . all to simply throw together something that would make people happy until such a day when Warner would unleash the film with the true respect it deserves.

"I am saddened to say that Warner themselves could not care less that I put this two-disc composite Special Edition bootleg out into the world (I did email them to let them know) but I am very happy to report that Shade Rupe informed Ken Russell of what I had done and Ken was delighted to know someone had taken it upon themselves to leak a composite of his masterpiece!"

It's in the wrong aspect ratio — the film was originally photographed in 2.35:1 Panavision, but is presented here in semi-widescreen release, 1.85:1 — and is grainy and washed-out-looking with some audio popping and hissing, but at least you can see the reassembled footage in the film.

But there's still no official release of the entire, uncut film although release dates come and go.

A release date of May 20, 2008, for an uncut 111-minute version of the film was announced and scuttled, and a cut version occasionally appears for download on iTunes — Guillermo del Toro told me, "I bought it twice [on iTunes]. I downloaded it to two different hard discs, because I said,

'What if they never release it again?' It was not the complete cut but nevertheless I try to see that movie at least every week . . . or portions of it." But according to a discouraged Russell, "You'll never see it the way I wanted you to. Never.

"It's not Warner's favorite movie, let's just put it that way," Russell told Total Sci-Fi On-Line in September 2010. "They won't release it. I'd like them to but they won't. And they aren't going to budge on that any time soon.

"They've just never liked it. It is as simple as that. They didn't like it back in 1971 and they don't like it today. They want nothing to do with it."

One reason Warners has backed off on the film is supplied by industry insider and proprietor of Hollywood Elsewhere .com Jeffrey Wells. In a blog entry dated March 29, 2010, he wrote, "An industry friend believes that 'one problem with *The Devils* is [Warner Brothers president and CEO] Alan Horn's overall conservatism, especially towards religion, as even *The Hangover* gave him problems, which is on record. So distributing a film on DVD that could incur the wrath of the religious right is not high on his agenda. He's a thought-police kind of guy who has major issues with raunch.'"

"I know Alan and he is very passionate about certain things," said Joe Dante when I raised the Alan Horn rumor. "Not [depicting] smoking in movies is one of them and he is in a position to assert his authority, so I wouldn't be surprised, knowing him, that this would be a picture he would be offended by."

When Russell was asked if he thought the film was blasphemous he replied with an emphatic no. "I never thought it was going to be called blasphemous. The critics just said that. And they were wrong. Warner might think it's blasphemous but I don't think it is. It is about a situation dating back hundreds of years. It is about the inability of sex and religion to marry. It is about sexual frustration and persecution."

He added that the pieces exist to create a fully uncensored, complete version of the film, the exact way he imagined it in 1971, but "Warner doesn't want to do it. It's a lost film now."

"I think this is a fairly popular topic at Warner Home Video," said Dante. "Whenever they have one of their online chats somebody always asks about *The Devils* and they always have to do some fancy footwork to not actually say it's never coming out but to dampen expectations.

"I think in today's climate it's a dicey item for them," Dante continues. "It is somewhat similar to the *Song of the South* situation at Disney. The people who will be offended will be very offended and are in a position to make a stink and of course, if you are a big company and you want to make a lot of money and make everybody happy and your image is important to you, I think the idea of being attacked by the religious right for releasing the movie on video is probably enough to make you take pause.

"Now, it's an embarrassment, frankly, for them. And it's an annoyance that these mosquito-like film buffs keep buzzing around their heads whining, 'When are you going to let us see it?' They really don't want to let us see it. They have no plans or intentions for us to see it. The people at Warner Home Video are not stupid. They're bright and they know people want to see this picture and I'm sure that within that organization there are people who are trying to figure out how to get the picture out. But it's a tough row to hoe when it has to get approval from upstairs."

Even the 2012 DVD release from BFI Video failed to get approval from the upper office types at Warner Brothers. Twitchfilm.com reported that the "rights for the film are held by Warner Brothers, and BFI has licensed the X-rated cut from them. Unfortunately, WB will not allow BFI or anyone else to release the film in its entirety at the moment.

Additionally, the licensors have prevented BFI from releasing the film on Blu-ray as well as denying them access to the 2004 restoration."

So four decades after its original release the movie is still too hot for the studio, but not for its fans, or for a new generation of critics who have widely praised the film, awarding it an 89% rating on Rotten Tomatoes.

English industrial metal band Godflesh uses the movie's themes as inspiration for many of their songs. "The one movie that's such a big influence on Godflesh is *The Devils*," says vocalist-guitarist Justin Broadrick, "particularly the first time we all saw it together on a lot of acid."

In 2007 visionary director Guillermo del Toro placed *The Devils* on a list alongside classics like *Nosferatu*, *City Lights* and James Whale's *Frankenstein* (Russell's *The Savage Messiah* also made the cut) for the Australian Centre for the Moving Image.

"I think that along with *Women in Love* it is the best Ken Russell film," del Toro told me in 2011. "[The way he portrayed] the political ferocity about the hypocrisy of the church, the marriage of church and state, the ultimate fallacy of the celibacy of priesthood, the mass hysteria and the political agenda of the destruction of the walls. You realize sort of the equivalent of shock doctrine through the possession. I thought it was incredibly smart.

"[It has a] great screenplay, incredibly quotable lines of dialogue, one of the three best performances Oliver Reed ever gave and one of the best performances Vanessa Redgrave ever gave. There's not a single bad actor in the bunch. And the music is perfect; this sort of concrete music that is creepy and unsettling."

Twelve years after he showed it on television Alex Cox was still tub-thumping for the film, placing it on a *Guardian* list of top films by independent British directors. At the time Cox wrote, "Who else would have dared such a thing? Who else but Russell — and his designer, Derek Jarman — could have pulled it off? Warning: this film may offend people of a religious (especially Christian) sensibility."

In 2011 when I asked him why it belongs on that list of the ten most important British films ever made he replied, "Those lists don't mean anything. I don't remember them. Why ten? Were they English-language films? How to decide such things?"

Despite his indifference to numerically ranking the art of Ken Russell, he had nothing but superlatives for the man himself. "He was one of the top men; up there with Lindsay Anderson and Kubrick and Nick Roeg. They and the young Tony Richardson were the greatest, most exciting generation of British directors."

Murray Melvin explained in 2011 that he and the film fans were "waging a campaign against Warner Brothers" to have the film released while Ken Russell, whose health was then failing, was still here to appreciate it. "It's got to be released before he goes," said Melvin. "He's got to go knowing that all those fans, those thousands of people worldwide, could be able to buy a copy."

"The people who were in charge at the time were horrified by the film," adds Ken Hanke, author of the 1984 book *Ken Russell's Films*. "Great. I can understand that. But how many of those people are still there?"

"As all film buffs know, if you burrow into the depths of Amazon.com you can probably find most movies that you want to see in some form or other," says Joe Dante, "but this is a movie that should not be seen on a dupey cassette. It is a movie that needs to be seen on a huge screen and it also needs to be seen with an audience because it is an audience film. When you see the film with an audience the reactions are palpable and they are varied but there's an electricity to the audience when they watch a picture like this because they've never seen anything like it. And it is very powerful."

In 2010 Chris Alexander, a longtime fan of the film ("*Dawn of the Dead*, *Night of the Hunter* and *The Devils* are my three favorite horror movies. I guess *Devils* and *Night* are not really horror movies by definition but certainly horrifying enough"), saw the movie with a sold-out audience of *Devils* newbies at the Fantasia festival in Montreal. I asked him about the film's appeal.

"On the surface there's the mystery and the mythology," he says, "people are really interested in turning over a rock and seeing what's underneath but I think it is one of those few movies that once you do uncover the rock, it actually pays off. It delivers."

It's impossible not to have a reaction to the film, even decades after it was made and that is, he suggests, one of the reasons it has been resurrected by festivals and audiences.

"It really confounded people," he says of the Montreal screening. "A lot of people came out hating it, which obviously is the greatest response. Whether you come out of *The Devils* swooning over it or despising it, the movie still is powerful. No one came out of that movie without a strong opinion about it."

Mitch Davis, head programmer for Fantasia, remembers the night. "Seeing [Russell] get three standing ovations by a crowd of seven hundred who were shrieking for him as though he were Mick Jagger was easily one of the most extraordinary experiences I've had in my entire curatorial career."

Murray Melvin chimes in, talking about a screening of the film in London. "At the Barbican the big number one cinema was full," he says. "We're talking 250, 300 people. Mostly young, middle-aged people. I mean, the standing ovation they gave Ken — [chokes up] sorry, it was just so tremendous. I hadn't seen it for a long time, but seeing it on the big screen . . . it really is unbelievably wonderful."

Judith Paris was also at the Barbican screening. "It was a very young audience who looked at it in astonishment. We have a very, very big immigrant community in London now and many of them were from other faiths and other cultures and I think they were completely bowled over by it. Completely staggered by it. I don't think they realized what they were actually going to be seeing. There was certainly a kind of stunned silence."

Once viewed — and while I'm no fan of bootleg films, this is a movie that demands to be seen by any means necessary — it is a film that cannot be forgotten or dismissed.

"Something like *The Devils* might actually cause some permanent damage [to audiences unprepared for its bombast]," says author Ken Hanke.

Maybe he's right, but until the film can be widely seen in its glorious, original uncut form, we'll never know for sure.

Appendix

HISTORICAL CAST OF CHARACTERS

Urbain Grandier
(Oliver Reed)

Urbain Grandier (1590–1634) served as a Catholic priest in the church of Sainte-Croix in Loudun, in the Diocese of Poitiers. He was a complicated man. In *Historic Ghosts and Ghost Hunters* author H. Addington Bruce says he was "frank and ardent and generous, and . . . idolized by the people of Loudun. But he had serious failings." A contemporary writer, Ismael Bouillau, said, "he had great virtues, but accompanied by great vices, human vices nevertheless, and natural to man." In other words, he was a horndog.

Writing in *Urbain Grandier, Celebrated Crimes*, the *Count of Monte Cristo* author Alexandre Dumas describes him thus: "Urbain, who in his intercourse with his friends was cordial and agreeable, was sarcastic, cold, and haughty to his enemies. When he had once resolved on a course, he pursued it unflinchingly; he jealously exacted all the honour due to the rank at which he had arrived, defending it as though it were a conquest; he also insisted on enforcing all his legal rights, and he resented the opposition and angry words of casual opponents with a harshness which made them his lifelong enemies."

One high-level enemy was the powerful Cardinal Richelieu. Grandier had both publicly spoken and published scathing criticisms against the chief minister of France. The result was a politically motivated witch hunt (literally) against Grandier led by Richelieu and his allies who used the priest's philandering lifestyle and bold affairs with women to impeach him. The strongest evidence came from the Mother Superior of the Ursuline nuns, Sister Jeanne of the Angels. Sister Jeanne, who was sexually obsessed with the priest, and felt jilted when he refused to become the spiritual director of the convent, accused him of using black magic to send the demon Asmodeus, among others, to seduce her and twenty-seven other nuns. That the nuns were cloistered and had never met the priest was incidental to the case.

Despite a paucity of hard evidence, and the fact that he never confessed to witchcraft, Grandier was found guilty and burned at the stake in the town square in August 1634.

The betrayal, trial and execution of Grandier have been widely documented in the years since. Alexandre Dumas detailed the story in volume four of his *Crimes Célèbres* (1840) and a play, *Urbain Grandier* (1850). French historian Jules Michelet discussed Grandier in a chapter of his book on the history of witchcraft, *La Sorcière* (1862), and Aldous Huxley told the sorry story in the 1952 book *The Devils of Loudun*.

Huxley's book was adapted for the stage by John Whiting (commissioned by the Royal Shakespeare Company) in 1961. Later that year it served as a basis for the Polish film *Matka Joanna od Aniołów* (*Mother Joan of the Angels*), directed by Jerzy Kawalerowicz. Later, in 1969, the story was adapted as an opera by Krzysztof Penderecki as *Die Teufel von Loudon*.

Jeanne des Anges
(Vanessa Redgrave)
In his definitive historical account of the possessions, *The Devils of Loudun*, Aldous Huxley writes, "Her name in religion was Jeanne des Anges; in the world it had been Jeanne de Belciel, daughter of Louis de Belciel, Baron de

Coze, and of Charlotte Goumart d'Eschillais, who came of a family hardly less ancient and eminent than his own. Born in 1602, she was now in her middle twenties, her face rather pretty, but her body diminutive almost to dwarfishness and slightly deformed — presumably by some tubercular infection of the bones. Jeanne's education had been only slightly less rudimentary than that of most young ladies of her time; but she was possessed of considerable native intelligence, combined, however, with a temperament and a character, which made her a trial to others and her own worst enemy."

Jeanne des Anges remained convinced of her saintliness until she died in 1665.

Father Pierre Barre
(Michael Gothard)

A specialist in exoticisms, Pierre Barre, the curate of Saint-Jacques in Chinon, arrived in Loudun on October 12, 1632. "This priest, whose name was Barre," wrote Alexandre Dumas, "was exactly the man whom Mignon needed in such a crisis. He was of melancholy temperament, and dreamed dreams and saw visions; his one ambition was to gain a reputation for asceticism and holiness."

In the film Barre appears to be a composite of the expert exorcists Capuchin Father Tranquille, Franciscan Father Lactance and Jesuit Father Jean-Joseph Surin. Late in the film Barre shatters Grandier's leg with a bootikens, a task performed in real life by Father Tranquille.

The undeniable psychosis Barre displays in the film also seems adapted from real life events. Grandier's three main tormentors all went downhill.

As the flames licked around him Grandier declared from his funeral pyre that Father Lactance, present, would die in thirty days. Thirty days later Father Lactance perished, uttering, "Grandier, I was not responsible for your death," before passing on to the long good night. (In the film Barre torments Grandier with a torch. "Confess! Confess! You have only a moment to live!" Grandier replies in much the same way his real life counterpart responded to Lactance. "Only a moment, but then I face the just and fearful judgment that you too, reverend father, will soon be called.")

Father Tranquille slipped into delirium several years afterwards, and Father Surin was haunted by the exorcisms to the point where he saw visions of demons with black wings and tried to kill himself.

Baron de Laubardemont
(Dudley Sutton)

Alexandre Dumas wrote that "every woodman needs an ax, every reaper a sickle, and Richelieu found the instrument he required in de Laubardemont, Councillor of State."

Baron Jean de Laubardemont, the Grand Admiral of France and His Majesty's Special Commissioner for the Destruction of the Fortifications of Loudun, was a distant relative of Sister Jeanne des Anges and a key figure in Richelieu's campaign of eliminating Huguenot influence by destroying local strongholds.

He was sent to Loudun to oversee the tearing down of the town's fortifications, but when stymied by the powerful Father Grandier he helped fabricate a case against him, coercing false statements of demonic possession from Sister Jeanne and the Ursuline nuns.

Through his efforts Grandier was executed and Loudun's walls were torn down. With them came tumbling down another Huguenot base ("Destroy the nests and the crows will disappear"), further strengthening his boss Cardinal Richelieu's power within the church and France.

The Devils of Loudun author Aldous Huxley notes that

while Baron de Laubardemont got away with his heinous behavior in Loudun, he was violently done in by highwaymen years later. "There must be a God," he wrote, "since this viper got it in the end after all."

Father Mignon
(Murray Melvin)

At the time of the possessions in Loudun Father Mignon, confessor to the Ursuline nuns, was in his eighties. In the film he's played by the thirty-nine-year-old Murray Melvin.

Described as "a zealous and learned ecclesiastic," in H. Addington Bruce's *Historic Ghosts and Ghost Hunters*, Mignon was also, according to Alexandre Dumas, "a revengeful, vindictive, and ambitious man; too commonplace ever to arrive at a high position, and yet too much above his surroundings to be content with the secondary position which he occupied."

His part in the story begins with a seemingly trivial matter, but as becomes obvious the more you study the tale, there is no such thing as a trivial matter in Loudun in the seventeenth century. Mignon enters after Grandier has unwittingly slighted Sister Jeanne by turning down the post of canon. Never having met Jeanne or been inside the convent Grandier had no idea that the Mother Superior was seriously obsessed with him, or that his rejection would be seen as a slap in the face.

Jeanne turned to Father Mignon, a man she knew disliked Grandier. He took the post and was soon hearing Jeanne's wild tales of sexual escapades and demonology. In the *Encyclopedia of Demons and Demonology*, author Rosemary Ellen Guiley says, "He became privy to the sexual secrets of the nuns, their nervous temperaments, and their ghost pranks in their haunted convent. It was soon easy to let them run out of control and become bewitched and beset by demons. Mignon conspired with Grandier's enemies to let it be known that he was responsible for their afflictions."

Cardinal Armand-Jean du Plessis de Richelieu (Christopher Logue)

The power-hungry Armand-Jean du Plessis, Cardinal-Duc de Richelieu et de Fronsac (1585–1642), was consecrated as a bishop in 1608 and within seventeen years became a cardinal and King Louis XIII's chief minister.

He is a main character in the retelling of the possessions at Loudun (and also features in *The Three Musketeers* by Alexandre Dumas, played by Charlton Heston in the film adaptation), and while he was a powerful man his hatred of Grandier stemmed from a trifling slight — a slight that ultimately cost Grandier everything.

Aldous Huxley reports that while at a religious convention in 1618, "Grandier went out of his way to offend the Prior of Coussay by rudely claiming precedence over him in a solemn procession through the streets of Loudun. Technically the parson's position was unassailable. In a procession originating in his own church, a Canon of Sainte-Croix had a right to walk in front of the Prior of Coussay. And this right held good even when, as was here the case, the Prior was at the same time a Bishop. But there is such a thing as courtesy; and there is also such a thing as circum-spection. The Prior of Coussay was the Bishop of Luçon, and the Bishop of Luçon was Armand-Jean du Plessis de Richelieu."

He waited years to exact his revenge but in 1633 issued this proclamation:

"Sieur de Laubardemont, Councillor of State and Privy Councillor, will betake himself to Loudun, and to what-ever other places may be necessary, to institute proceedings against Grandier on all the charges formerly preferred against him, and on other facts which have since come to light, touching the possession by evil spirits of the Ursuline nuns of Loudun, and of other persons, who are said likewise to be tormented of devils through the evil practices of the said Grandier; he will diligently investigate everything from the beginning that has any bearing either on the said possession or on the exorcisms, and will forward to us his report thereon, and the reports and other documents sent in by former commissioners and delegates, and will be present at all future exorcisms, and take proper steps to obtain evidence of the said facts, that they may be clearly established; and, above all, will direct, institute, and carry through the said proceedings against Grandier and all others who have been involved with him in the said case, until definitive sentence be passed; and in spite of any appeal or countercharge this cause will not be delayed (but without prejudice to the right of appeal in other causes), on account of the nature of the crimes, and no regard will be paid to any request for postponement made by the said Grandier. His majesty commands all governors, provincial lieutenant-generals, bailiffs, seneschals, and other municipal authorities, and all subjects whom it may concern, to give every assistance in arresting and imprisoning all persons whom it may be necessary to put under constraint, if they shall be required so to do."

King Louis XIII
(Graham Armitage)

Taking the throne at only nine years of age, Louis XIII was a Bourbon monarch who ruled as King of France and of Navarre from 1610 until his death from complications of intestinal tuberculosis in 1643. In 1617 he exiled his mother, Marie de Medici, and executed her followers because of political intrigue and their mismanagement of his kingdom. Aloof and skeptical by nature, he relied heavily on his most trusted advisor Cardinal Richelieu to do the day-to-day governing of the kingdom although final say on any matter always rested with the king.

Madeleine de Brou
(Gemma Jones)

Madeleine de Brou, the orphaned daughter of a royal councilor, was Urbain Grandier's mistress and, later, his wife. They were wed in a secret ceremony, and the news of the nuptials is one of the key elements that drive the lovesick Sister Jeanne to betray Grandier.

Grandier and de Brou's relationship was the subject of much gossip in Loudun and it was rumored that he had penned "a little handwritten book against the celibacy of priests," addressed to "his dearest concubine." Later, during the trial, two of her brothers would become steadfast supporters of Grandier.

Sister Agnes
(Judith Paris)

Agnes was Cardinal Richelieu's niece, allegedly placed in the convent by the cardinal to act as a spy to dig up dirt on Sister Jeanne, the Mother Superior of the newly minted Ursulines of the Roman Union.

According to *The Encyclopedia of Demons and Demonology* by Rosemary Ellen Guiley, "The Ursuline convent was new, established in 1626 by seventeen nuns, most of them of noble birth. They were not particularly pious but were sent to the convent because their families could not afford dowries large enough to attract suitors of comparable rank. Most were resigned to their fate and lived lives of boredom at the convent."

Sister Agnes provided little useful intelligence to her uncle, aside from learning that Sister Jeanne was completely mad.

In the film Sister Agnes's most recognizable line comes early on as Grandier parades through the town. Perched in the convent window she gushes, "Yes! I can see him! He is the most beautiful man in the world!"

Louis Trincant
(John Woodvine)

Louis Tricant was the king's prosecutor at the royal courts of Loudun, a deputy of the Tiers-États at the États Généraux of 1614. He was also a historian and author of *Histoire généalogique de la Maison de Savonnières en Anjou* and several polemical tracts dedicated to Richelieu.

Philippe Trincant
(Georgina Hale)

Philippe Trincant was born in October 1603. She was twenty-one, thirteen years younger than Grandier, when she had an illegitimate relationship with him that resulted in a child. Her birth records are held at Loudun but she was actually born at Thouars, fifteen miles from there. The details of the birth of her illegitimate child with Grandier are foggy, having been hushed up by her powerful father. In *A Case of Witchcraft*, author Robert Rapley says, "In September 1629 Tricant wrote a letter to his great friends the Sainte-Marthe brothers, saying that Grandier's once great reputation had been destroyed some eight months earlier, which indicates that the conception took place around that time, ie: between January and March 1629."

Ibert
(Max Adrian)

As well as shaving and haircutting, barber-surgeons (also known as surgeons of the short robe) in seventeenth-century France performed medical treatments such as bloodletting, tooth drawing, cauterization and tending to other minor injuries and wounds. Ibert, played by Max Adrian, would have been a barber, employed to provide a "scientific" approach to Grandier ("No blood when the tongue was pricked, true sign of the devil," he says during Grandier's torture) and Sister Jeanne's intrusive interrogations.

In an essay titled "The Barber Pole," Harry Perelman, M.D., points out that "the origin of the barber pole appears to be associated with the service of bloodletting. The original pole had a brass basin at the top representing the vessel in which leeches were kept, and also representing the basin which received the blood. The pole itself represents the staff which the patient held onto during the procedure." Once the operation was complete the barber-surgeon would hang the both bloodstained and clean bandages on the staff to dry and attract customers. The wind would twist the bandages into the pattern we now recognize as the modern-day barber pole.

Sympathy for The Devils

A CONVERSATION WITH GUILLERMO DEL TORO

Guillermo del Toro is many things. The Mexican-born filmmaker is an Oscar nominee for his screenplay to Pan's Labyrinth, *a novelist, movie producer, designer and, of course, the visionary director behind the films* The Devil's Backbone, Hellboy *and* Pacific Rim. *He's also a Ken Russell fan who calls* The Devils *a "grand masterwork." Taking a break from his busy schedule, del Toro spoke with me about Russell, Reed, Redgrave and how* The Devils *ruffled the feathers of almost everyone who saw it.*

RC: What did you think of *Raising Hell*?

GDT: I loved it. I thought I knew everything about the movie and I was wrong.

RC: When did you first become aware of *The Devils* movie and Ken Russell?

GDT: I actually became aware of Ken Russell through *The Devils*. I read the book — *The Devils of Loudon* — right after seeing the movie. Fortunately for me it was in print in Spanish. I used to love the movie. I saw it on VHS, on those big clunky boxes that Warner Brothers used to put out in the early days of VHS. It became a treasured possession. I wore it down. There was a time — I have nothing left now — when I was able to recite almost the entire movie's dialogue. I read the book after and it gave a new meaning to the movie. I started extrapolating stuff that was fascinating; like, I love the idea that Aldous Huxley mentions the anal fistulas that Richelieu has that impeded his movement. He was mostly supported by acolytes because he couldn't walk and I thought Ken Russell did it beautifully with that wheelbarrow. It's a very smart supposition. In Huxley it's a very tragic piece of biography but what is great about Ken Russell is, here is the most powerful man in France and he is potentially unable to walk. It is the ultimate perversion.

RC: Ken always said that this movie was historically accurate and if people were offended by the film then they were offended by history.

GDT: In a funny way even the arrogance and entitlements of vulgarity are so well portrayed. It is so well portrayed that medical science is arrogant in the movie. Political powers are arrogant in the movie, and ultimately they destroy not only the walls but what seems to be the only or one of the few thinking men that is accused of arrogance and is accused of communing with the devil but is really a very touching character. Grandier is a very beautifully vulnerable human being. That's why Oliver Reed is so perfect. I always saw him like a living, breathing Auguste Rodin sculpture. The epitome of humanity made flesh.

RC: It is his eyes that grab me. You can't avoid his gaze.

GT: He was a guy that, in my opinion, had an incredible vibration of emotion in his voice at all times. He had a timbre and a tremolo in his voice that always signaled huge emotion for me. The other thing that he did well is the position of his body, of that incredible physicality with the illusion of vulnerability. He did it on this movie. He did it on *Curse of the Werewolf* and he did it his best roles, like *Women in Love*. You understood that this mountain of a man was vulnerable and emotional. It's quite a singular screen presence he had.

RC: I can't imagine anyone else playing that role. Alan Bates, Richard Burton, Richard Harris . . .

GDT: I say that Oliver Reed is one of the best actors to sweat. When you see him perspire . . . it's an extremely elegant display of sweat dropping. You understand his turmoil better than ever. No one else could do that supposition of power and fragility.

RC: What do you think of Vanessa Redgrave in this movie?

GDT: I think she's perfect. In my opinion it is one of her best roles ever. She has just the exact touch of the thin lips, the hysterical eyes, to be a very beautiful nun, and Mother Jeanne of Angels is described in the book as a woman who had a very fair, delicate beautiful face but was disfigured by the hump. I think Redgrave has this face that is at the same time beautiful and puritanical, you know? She can also express incredible fires of desire but she still has in her face and in her features a certain sternness. A certain steeliness. I think there is not a single miscast character in the movie. It is one of my favorite movies of all time.

RC: Is it true you watch at least part of the movie every week?

GDT: I used to. Now that the new DVD has come out I find that that is true again. But for a while I would watch it at least once every thirty, forty days. There are three movies of Ken Russell's that I adore. I love all of them, but I adore *Women in Love, The Devils* and *Savage Messiah*. For me those are the top three, and I try to watch them as often as possible. He was a singular mind and I wish I had met him . . . I met him once in Telluride but he was not very social.

He was a singular mind with a singular eye and he had such a powerful style that whether his movies hit or miss there is still a beautiful alchemy between his style and the material. My fourth favorite movie of his, which is *Mahler*, comes close for me to the others but is not as powerful for me, but when he marries the material . . . I think the supreme marriage of material is in the top three [films] because they articulate a credo of what he thinks life is. *Women in Love* articulates the essential maleness and an essential male point of view. *Savage Messiah* is almost a manifest about how an artist has to be an iconoclast and how an artist has to be savage and indomitable, and then *The Devils* shows the absolute insanity that it is to try to remain rational when the forces of time and history are against you. He was hugely influential for me in terms of composition, the way he made everything fall into place when it seemed impossible. I think he's unique in cinema.

RC: Do you think his work, because of all you've just said, and *The Devils* specifically, influenced your work and the way you work today?

GDT: One thing that is curious is that I'm influenced more by his quiet moments than I am influenced by his gyrating camera. You know that crazier camera? What he did that I think is fantastic and that I tried to [emulate] is that he sustained the marriage of pain and beauty — opposites, like water and oil — by tone. He had such an overlaying tone on everything he touched. If you saw those pieces of film individually — I can't imagine seeing the dailies — there are moments of quote, unquote, I would say, *normalcy* that are so high pitched. The actors are reciting the dialogue at a burning pace, seemingly overacting, the camera is zooming back and forth or sweeping across the frame, and yet those little mosaics of madness fit perfectly. Then he always has the serenity — the confidence, rather — to snap back from those moments of great madness and show you moments of absolute serenity.

RC: Why do you think this movie still enrages people? The new BFI DVD doesn't even have all the scenes.

GDT: It is almost like a reversal of what Ken Russell said. He said that people in the past never think they are living in a historical time. That they see themselves as completely modern and their hang-ups and backwards ways become exposed by history. You can laugh and chuckle at the science exposed in the movie, which is as close to witchcraft as anything else, and you can laugh at the fact that you can whip up a religious frenzy with just a few elements like that, but then you look at us and we are still upset at a piece of film. We are still, in essence — in regards to religion, sadly — still very much in the Middle Ages. Our relationship with God and the universe, for a majority of people, is still one of complete verticality and, in the worst possible way, blind faith. To me the movie is both spiritual and political, and in both incidences it is an incredibly subversive film. In both incidences we are still in the Middle Ages. Particularly in the religious aspect. I mean the fact that this movie, to this day, after his death, is not properly released to the world, the way he saw it, the way he wanted it, I think actually the world has taken a step backwards. If you think about the particular case of this movie there is a character who is, I don't think, available socially to anyone anymore, and that is a thinking censor. Censorship that may not be honorable, or may not be brave or anything like that, but was at least able to acknowledge the power of the film. Whereas now the film is viewed with either absolute devotion — like I have or Mark Kermode has or you have — or an almost animalistic horror. I know people who hate the movie and have never seen it.

RC: The *idea* of this movie enrages people so much. Hopefully the book can convince people that this is a movie that is a brave and individualistic work of art from a film-maker, the kinds of which we don't have anymore.

GDT: Think about two things. One, I'm a lapsed Catholic, but one of the most religious and moving films about the life of Christ is *The Last Temptation of Christ*, the Scorsese movie. It outraged the right-wing Catholics and Christians, and when you see the movie, it is such an incredibly powerful statement of faith and such a monumental shrine to the man. This movie actually shows you the true fountain of serenity and faith in Grandier. The intimate moments of communion that he has apart from the maddening noise of the world. That moment of serenity that is perfectly juxtaposed with the hysterics — it's a moment, that if anything, speaks volumes about what a true Catholic or Christian should be able to do. And the second thing that is amazing to me is that this movie is essentially showing you, centuries ago, showing you exactly how many are still inactive in the great social changes, which is the Shock Doctrine. They are doing essentially the Shock Doctrine through the exorcisms. They distract the masses with something really, really big that we create and orchestrate so while they're looking that way we can pass this huge, damaging social change measure.

They will not notice because they will be so happy to have witnessed the end of something so bad. Naomi Klein would be absolutely in awe of Richelieu. What I'm trying to say is, if you need any more proof that we're still in the Middle Ages you need to look no further.

This is the perfect time. I do believe Ken Russell was a filmmaker who was savagely neglected by a lot of the film community who seem to think his films are dated and a lot of them aren't. Some of them are, but a lot of them aren't. Not that it mattered to him, because he was an iconoclast. He was an *enfant terrible.* He was a rebel and he didn't really need the accolades that much, but he needed the financing. He needed distribution and he needed production and all those things were terribly neglected to him. In a way I find the same type of mythology has hit Terry Gilliam.

I think Ken Russell really ruffled the feathers of a lot of a) the religious establishment, b) the social conservatives and c) a body of critics that were, frankly, retrograde. That were looking for a different system of values from the ones that Ken Russell was able to articulate. Let me put it this way: his body of work is enviable. *Enviable.* The cohesiveness is absolutely enviable.

RC: Do you think a movie like this could get made today?

GDT: Not at all. Not at all for one reason. For one reason only. The story could be told, but the budget . . . it's a big movie. It's a movie that has some of the most beautiful and complex sets by Derek Jarman that occupied a large portion of the studio. Now if you wanted to build a set that size, the scale and almost monolithic nature of the city, you couldn't do it because you'd need a budget and there is no financing entity in the world today who would take a risk like that. It only makes us much more of a sadder culture really.

RC: Joe Dante told me that the only way this movie could get made today is if there was an insane millionaire willing to pick up the tab.

GDT: And they are few and far apart.

RC: I think Derek Jarman is fifty percent responsible for the visual success of this film.

GDT: I agree. Those sets are incredible but funny enough I'll tell you this as a director, they are sets that are not easy to photograph. They are sets from aspect. First of all is the fact that white is incredibly hard to work with. Black and white that close to the human faces. The fact that if you don't use the right composition and right kind of wide angle lens you're not going to get the majesty of those sets. I believe it was a very fleeting but happy marriage of two geniuses. You're lighting white and you're lighting black and you're lighting the human faces and you have things standing together that are several steps apart from each other. I find it breathtaking and I strive all my life to have an opening shot as powerful as the opening shot of *The Devils*. I think in cinematic terms, the stark elegance of Jarman gives a certain gravitas to the things that are happening on screen that would be absent if you had a more realistic production design.

RC: Or if they were busier. Because the sets are white and stark they force my eye to the actors.

GDT: It tells you these are the characters standing in their epoch, in their time. You are trapped in the surroundings but you can put yourself in those characters.

RC: You said earlier that all the characters are perfectly cast. I particularly like de Laubardemont. He is one of the great villains.

GDT: He is amazing and his face is so expressive. He is really one of the great villains and Father Barre . . . a lot of people complain about him with his John Lennon glasses and the Andy Warhol type of character, but I think that is exactly right. That's the only way we can relate to him. There's a thing that happens. People look at religious paintings from the Renaissance and from medieval times and in a lot of them people are standing in contemporary clothes in the paintings. They are not people in period garb but when you look at them from the twentieth century the past is the past, but that is the brilliance of Ken Russell. He is bringing these contemporary culture touches to make the characters more accessible.

RC: In some ways that's our doorway into the story. The story is complicated so you have to have very human characters as the entry point for the viewer into this intense story.

GDT: That is exactly what I'm saying about Father Barre. The brilliant thing is when you watch it and you realize he moves like a rock star, or he moves like Andy Warhol or John Lennon, it's a concert. It's show time. The hysteria of the audience and the nuns is the same hysteria you would have had in the 1970s at the height of a huge concert. The nudity. The frenzy, the lasciviousness, the freedom, the madness. It is a really interesting supposition that he outs this rock star priest in the middle of this thing.

RC: The first time I saw him I thought Mick Jagger.

GDT: Yeah, yeah. He has the strut of a rock star. The delivery of a rock star. The hair and lips of a rock star.

RC: What do you think about the burning at the stake scene? A number of people I've talked to who haven't seen the movie for a very long time, the scene they always come back to is the burning at the stake scene. I can't think of another burning at the stake scene, previous to *The Devils*, that depicted it in such a vivid way.

GDT: I would agree with you. What *The Devils* does is that it really shows you not only the stake but breaking his feet and legs is really excruciating and he lives through it. He becomes a martyr. He becomes, I would not say a messiah, because he really does not save anyone but it's like Jesus being crucified by the Romans. Being charged in the Roman court. In other words it becomes a passion play. In order for it to become a passion play these very saintly people have to be in essence crucifying a saint. Not a saint in the moral sense but certainly a messiah, a man who had a message. In the name of the messiah they are crucifying another one, and one of the essential things in the narrative of Jesus is the minute description of the torture, the minute detail of a forensic nature of his suffering. I think that the great, great difference that is very shocking at the end between Jesus and Grandier is the blackened bones. The blackened bones are such a brutal, concrete material reminder that this is not just a tragedy of the spirit, it is a tragedy of the material world. The perfect, rhythmic, symphonic marriage of his blackened bones and the destruction of the white walls is utterly fascinating to me because the movie has utilized those two colors throughout the film and the coda to those colors is the bone used as a dildo and the blackened bones in contrast of the destroyed white walls. It is beyond meaning and just a pure sheer artistic gesture. It's amazing.

The fact that one of the bones is used as a dildo is absolutely . . . it shows you in many ways the absolutely sterile necrophiliac nature of the passion of Mother Jeanne of Angels. The word *genius* is so overused and is used in connection, most of the time, with *overrated* . . . Ken Russell and *The Devils* is sheer genius.

RC: The word masterpiece is overused as well. Do you think it is going too far to call this Ken Russell's masterpiece?

GDT: No. I would agree with you. I would agree with you because the other two I love, which are *Women in Love* and *Savage Messiah*, have a more minor tone. I think tonally this is his grand work. Tonally this is his grand masterwork. It is a movie that is ambitious, symphonic and, in my opinion, absolutely perfect.

BIBLIOGRAPHY

"Alexander Walker, Film critic for the Evening Standard who held the British film industry to account for more than 40 years." The *Times*. <www.timesonline.co.uk/tol/comment/obituaries/article1151392.ece>. July 2003.

Atkins, Thomas R., ed. *Ken Russell*. New York: Simon & Shuster, 1976.

Balz, Adam. "*The Devils*." <notcoming.com/reviews/thedevils/>. 2010.

Baxter, John. *An Appalling Talent: Ken Russell*. London: Michael Joseph Ltd., 1973.

Berkeley, Michael. "Mr. Unstoppable." The *Guardian*. <www.guardian.co.uk/music/2004/mar/09/classicalmusicandopera3>. March 2004.

Brooke, Michael. "Amelia and the Angel." ScreenOnline. <www.screenonline.org.uk/film/id/442042>.

Cashill, Robert. "Downloading *The Devils*." Between Productions. <robertcashill.blogspot.com/2010/06/downloading-devils.html>. June 19, 2010.

Cawthorne, Nigel. *The Who and the Making of* Tommy. London: Unanimous Ltd., 2005.

Conrich, Ian. "Film Classification and the BBFC." BBC Online. <www.bbc.co.uk/films/2000/09/26/film_classification_article.shtml>. October 2003.

De Certeau, Michel. *The Possession at Loudun*, trans. Michael B. Smith. Chicago: The University of Chicago Press, 1996.

De Plancy, Collin. *Dictionary of Witchcraft*, trans. Wade Baskin. New York: Philosophical Library, Inc., 1965.

de Rosée, Sophie. "Ken Russell, filmmaker: The 83-year-old filmmaker discusses naked wrestling, ballet and his conversations with God." The *Telegraph*. <www.telegraph.co.uk/culture/film/7863070/Ken-Russell-filmmaker.html>. June 30, 2010.

"*The Devils* Case Study." Students' British Board of Film Classification. <www.sbbfc.co.uk/CaseStudies/The_Devils>.

"Director in a Caftan." *Time* magazine. <www.time.com/time/magazine/article/0,9171,903120,00.html>. September 1971.

Dumas, Alexandre. *Celebrated Crimes*. The Literature Network. <www.online-literature.com/dumas/celebrated-crimes/40/>.

Fielder, Harry Aitch. "1971 *The Devils*." Turnipnet. <www.turnipnet.com/aitch/aitch/1971.htm>.

Fisher, Iain. "Wynn Wheldon interviewed by Iain Fisher about his father Huw Wheldon." Iainfisher.com. <www.iainfisher.com/russell/ken-russell-article-wheldon.html>.

Flatley, Guy. "He Was Surprised That His Films Shocked People — Or So He Said." Movie Crazed. <www.moviecrazed.com/outpast/russellken.html>.

Galt, John. "Psychological Interpretation of the Film *The Devils*." Yahoo! Voices. <www.associatedcontent.com/article/370688/psychological_interpretation_of_the_pg4.html?cat=9>. September 2007.

Gomez, Joseph. *Ken Russell: The Adapter as Creator*. London: Frederick Muller Limited, 1976.

Goodwin, Cliff. *Evil Spirits: The Life of Oliver Reed*. London: Virgin Books Ltd, 2001.

Greydanus, Steven D. "The Devil in Tinsel Town." *Christianity Today*. <www.christianitytoday.com/ct/

movies/commentaries/2011/deviltinseltown.html>.
January 2011.

Hanke, Ken. "*The Devils.*" Mountain XPress. <www.
mountainx.com/movies/review/devils#.ToSu9Il2zZU>.
April 2007.
Harrison, David. "15 Things You Genuinely Didn't Know
About Oliver Reed." Bubblegun. <www.bubblegun.
com/features/15oliver.html>. May 12, 2000.
Hauptfuhrer, Fred. "Ken & Shirley Russell: He Directed
Tommy, Her Job Is Even Tougher, Directing
Him." *People*. <www.people.com/people/archive/
article/0,,20065536,00.html>. August 1975.
Hays, Matthew. "Altered statesman." *Montreal Mirror*.
<www.montrealmirror.com/2010/071510/film1.html>.
July 2010.
Huxley, Aldous. *The Devils of Loudun*. New York: Harper
& Brothers, 1952.

Jarman, Derek. *Dancing Ledge*. Minneapolis: University of
Minneapolis Press, 2010.

Kermode, Mark. *The Exorcist*, Revised Second Edition.
London: British Film Institute, 2011.
Kermode, Mark. *It's Only a Movie: Reel Life Adventures
if a Film Obsessive*. London: Random House Books,
2010.
Kermode, Mark. "The Devil Himself: Ken Russell." Video
Watchdog. No. 35, 1996, pp. 51–56.

Lanza, Joseph. *Phallic Frenzy: Ken Russell and his Films*.
Chicago: Chicago Review Press, 2007.
Lethem, Jonathan. *They Live: A Novel Approach to
Cinema*. Berkley: Soft Skull Press, 2010.

Lister, David. "Russell's 'rape of Christ' to be shown." *Independent.* <www.independent.co.uk/news/media/russells-rape-of-christ-to-be-shown-604844.html>. November 20, 2002.

Lucas, Tim. "Cutting the Hell Out of *The Devils.*" *Video Watchdog.* No. 35, 1996, pp. 36-51.

Luck, Richard. "Ken Russell: The Old Devil." Sabotage Times. <www.sabotagetimes.com/tv-film/ken-russell-the-old-devil/>. September 2011.

Lyons, Kevin. "*The Devils* Review." The Encyclopedia of Fantastic Film and Television. <www.eofftv.com/review/d/devils_review.htm>. January 2009.

Moore, Kieron. "Ten Divine Cinematic Priests." The Film Pilgrim. <www.thefilmpilgrim.com/features/ten-divine-cinematic-priests/3384>. May 2011.

Moore, Less Lee. "Now There's A Man Worth Going To Hell For: *The Devils* And Ken Russell." Pop Shifter. <popshifter.com/2010-09-29/now-theres-a-man-worth-going-to-hell-for-the-devils-and-ken-russell/>. September 2010.

"Opera: The Devil and Penderecki." *Time* magazine. <www.time.com/time/magazine/article/0,9171,840198,00.html>. July 4, 1969.

Phillips, Gene D. "A Blast from the Past: An Interview with Ken Russell." *Film Comment.* <www.filmlinc.com/film-comment/article/a-blast-from-the-past-an-interview-with-ken-russell>.

Rees, Jasper. "theartsdesk Q&A: Director Ken Russell." The Arts Desk. <www.theartsdesk.com/film/theartsdesk-qa-director-ken-russell>. June 19, 2010.

Rule, Vera. "Shirley Russell: Ken shot the movies, she dressed his stars in a variety of weird and wonderful outfits." The *Guardian*. <www.guardian.co.uk/news/2002/mar/22/guardianobituaries>. March 22, 2002.

Russell, Ken. "The Best of Ken Russell." The *Times*. <www.timesonline.co.uk/tol/system/topicRoot/Ken_Russell/>. November 28, 2010.

Russell, Ken. *Directing Film: The Director's Art from Script to Cutting Room*. Washington: Brassey's Inc., 2001.

Russell, Ken. *A British Picture, An Autobiography*. London: Mandarin, 1989.

Russell, Ken. *Altered States*. New York: Bantam Books, 1991.

Spalding. John D. "What If Satan Were One of Us?" BeliefNet.com. <www.beliefnet.com/Entertainment/2000/09/What-If-Satan-Were-One-Of-Us.aspx>. November, 2000.

Trevelyan, John. *What the Censor Saw*. London: Michael Joseph Ltd, 1973.

Vermilye, Jerry. "Alan Bates, D.H. Lawrence's counterpart in both philosophy and physical likeness, is at his best in a vivid display of lighthearted cynicism . . ." AlanBates.com. <alanbates.com/abarchive/film/wil.html>. November 1999.

Waddell, Calum. "Ken Russell: Devils Worship." Total Sci-fi Online. <totalscifionline.com/interviews/5545-ken-russell-devils-worship>. September 28, 2010.

Wells, Jeffrey. "A History of Censorship." Hollywood Elsewhere. <hollywood-elsewhere.com/2010/03/a_ history_of_ce.php>. March 29, 2010.

Weirdmoviebuff. "The Wild World of Ken Russell." Weird Movie Village. <www.weirdmovievillage.com/2010/11/ wild-world-of-ken-russell.html>. November 28, 2010.

Wilkinson, Carl, ed. *The Observer Book of Film*. London: Observer Books, 2007.

RICHARD CROUSE is the regular film critic for CTV's *Canada AM* and CTV's 24-hour News Channel. His syndicated Saturday afternoon radio show, *Entertainment Extra*, originates on NewsTalk 1010. He is also the author of six books on pop culture history including *Who Wrote the Book of Love* and *The 100 Best Movies You've Never Seen*, and writes two weekly columns for *Metro* newspaper. He lives in Toronto, Ontario.

At ECW Press, we want you to enjoy this book in whatever format you like, whenever you like. Leave your print book at home and take the eBook to go! Purchase the print edition and receive the eBook free. Just send an email to ebook@ecwpress.com and include:

• the book title
• the name of the store where you purchased it
• your receipt number
• your preference of file type: PDF or ePub?

A real person will respond to your email with your eBook attached. Thank you for supporting an independently owned publisher with your purchase!

Get the
eBook
free!